Information Technology Systems

BTEC Level 3 National in Information Technology
Unit 1 Information Technology Systems

P.M. Heathcote

Published by
PG Online Limited
The Old Coach House
35 Main Road
Tolpuddle
Dorset
DT2 7EW
United Kingdom
sales@pgonline.co.uk
www.pgonline.co.uk
2019

PG ONLINE

Pearson Endorsement Statement

Acknowledgements

Every effort has been made to trace and acknowledge ownership of copyright. The publishers will be happy to make any future amendments with copyright owners. The author and publisher would like to thank the following companies and individuals who granted permission for the use of their images in this textbook.

Chapter 1
Amazon Go © Erica.com / Shutterstock.com

Chapter 2
Self-service checkouts © photocritical / Shutterstock.com

Chapter 3
Sip puff device and foot operated mouse © Inclusive Technology Ltd
Amazon Echo © pianodiaphragm / Shutterstock.com

Chapter 6
WinZip screenshots © Corel Corporation

Chapter 9
Cable laying © Tove Valley Broadband

Chapter 14
Food truck © Blulz60 / Shutterstock.com

Chapter 15
Sage screenshot © The Sage Group plc

Chapter 17
Wikipedia screen shot © pixinoo / Shutterstock.com

Chapter 18
Social media buttons © Hadrian / Shutterstock.com

Chapter 25
Android layout visualiser © Udacity Labs
Grocery delivery van © Martin Hoscik / Shutterstock.com

Chapter 28
British Gas questionnaire © Centrica plc
Amazon homescreen © littlenySTOCK / Shutterstock.com

Chapter 31
TeleGeography 2018 Global Internet Map © TeleGeography, www.telegeography.com
Malawi school © David Ames
Planting potatoes in Idaho © B Brown/ Shutterstock
Environmental pollution © Stephen Gibson/ Shutterstock

Chapter 32
Prison interior © photocritical / Shutterstock.com

Chapter 34
Sir Tim Berners-Lee © drserg / Shutterstock.com
Screenshots of Microsoft Office products © Microsoft

Preface

The aim of this book is to provide comprehensive coverage of topics in Unit 1 of the BTEC Level 3 course in Information Technology in an interesting and approachable manner. If you are studying this course, you need to notice, read about, experience and analyse the impact and implications of current and emerging digital technologies. This text is not intended to be merely a reference manual, but rather as an approach to teaching and learning. Examples and case studies from scenarios and events that have recently been in the news are used to bring the subject to life. Reading and discussing articles from quality newspapers, whether printed or online, discussing relevant TV documentaries, noticing and analysing the use of digital technology in countless aspects of life, as well as learning from a textbook, are all going to contribute to a successful exam result.

The book is divided into six sections corresponding to the six Learning Aims outlined in the specification. These sections are divided into between four and eight chapters, each containing material that can be covered in one or two lessons. The chapters have in-text questions which can be used as discussion points in a lesson. An extra chapter at the end of Learning Aim B on "Drawing System Diagrams" will be useful for students faced with a question on the exam for which they are required to draw such a diagram.

Topics are covered usually, but not always, in the same order as the specification, with some subsections of the specification spread over two chapters. Sometimes the material is covered in a different sequence from that given in the specification in order to give a better overall view of a particular topic.

This unit is externally assessed through a written examination set and marked by Pearson. In the final assessment, each of the questions in the exam will require a good grasp of several areas of the specification, so all chapters in the book need to be carefully studied and revised.

In addition to almost 100 in-text questions and discussion points, there are over 80 end-of-chapter exercises that are designed to give practice in answering exam-style questions, using command words such as **state**, **describe**, **explain**, **analyse**. As much practice as possible is needed in answering such questions and getting feedback from the teacher so as to understand how to gain the maximum possible marks in the final exam. Answers to all questions and exercises are available to teachers only in a free Teacher's Pack which can be ordered from our website **www.pgonline.co.uk.**

First edition 2019

A catalogue entry for this book is available from the British Library

ISBN: 978-1-910523-15-5

Contents

Unit 1: Information Technology Systems

		Pack A	Pack B	Pack C	Pack D	Pack E	Pack F
Learning Aim A: Digital devices in IT systems							
A1	Digital devices, their functions and use	✓					
A2	Peripheral devices and media	✓					
A3	Computer software in an IT system	✓					
A4	Emerging technologies	✓					
A5	Choosing IT systems	✓					
Learning Aim B: Transmitting data							
B1	Connectivity		✓				
B2	Networks		✓				
B3	Issues relating to transmission of data		✓				
Learning Aim C: Operating online							
C1	Online systems			✓			
C2	Online communities			✓			
Learning Aim D: Protecting data and information							
D1	Threats to data, information and systems				✓		
D2	Protecting data				✓		
Learning Aim E: Impact of IT systems							
E1	Online services					✓	
E2	Impact on organisations					✓	
E3	Using and manipulating data					✓	
Learning Aim F: Issues							
F1	Moral and ethical issues						✓
F2	Legal issues						✓

LEARNING AIM A
Digital devices in IT Systems

In this section:

Chapter 1
Digital devices

Objectives

- Describe digital devices that form part or all of IT systems:
  - multifunctional devices
  - personal computers
  - mobile devices
  - servers
  - entertainment systems
  - digital cameras – still, video
  - navigation systems
  - data capture and collection systems
  - communication devices and systems

An information technology system

An **IT system** refers to all the hardware and software used for a particular purpose. A small business may have a single IT system comprising several networked PCs, a server, and several software packages for carrying out the various tasks that the business performs to keep everything running smoothly. A large organisation may have hundreds of computing devices linked in a network, and several sub-systems each designed to carry out different functions.

 Describe some of the hardware and software making up the IT system at your school or college. List the different categories of users; for example, teaching staff and students. Do some departments have specialised IT equipment and software?

This chapter is a short overview of some of the digital devices that are used in different ways by organisations and individuals.

Multifunctional devices

Multifunctional devices, as the name suggests, are used for a multitude of different functions. In an office or school environment, for example, most deskwork will be done using a desktop computer, which would typically be either a PC or Apple iMac. Many people working at home or while travelling to and from work use a laptop.

Here is a comparison:

Desktop	Laptop
Generally have more powerful processors for a lower price	Originally less powerful and more expensive but becoming more powerful and cheaper
Easier to expand, modify and upgrade	Have batteries and can be used where there is no power supply
Screen is at eye level and user can work with a better posture	Incorporate peripherals such as speakers and microphones which do not have to be bought separately
Less easy to steal and carry away	Portable and can be used in different locations
Have powerful GPUs (Graphics Processing Unit) for manipulating and editing images	

Smartphones, cellular networks and tethering a smartphone to a laptop are discussed in Chapters 10 and 11 of Learning Aim B.

Servers

In most organisation with more than two or three computers, the computers will be networked. The most common form of network is a client-server network, described in Learning Aim B, Chapter 11. Such a network will have at least one server, holding and managing data for all the client computers. There may be a separate web server, mail server and print server or these functions may be combined in a single hardware device.

A server is a fast, powerful computer with extensive storage capacity. In a small network, the server will not look much different from the main processor box, containing the CPU and disk drive, supplied with a powerful PC. In a large network, the file servers could occupy acres of space for data storage.

Entertainment systems

A home entertainment system may refer to:

- a home cinema that reproduces a movie theatre experience, using video and audio equipment
- a desktop computer with software applications supporting video and music playback and games software

What features would you look for in a PC that was going to be used for playing games software?

A PC can be used as an entertainment system allowing a user to:

- watch cable and satellite television stations
- record, pause and play back digital content
- watch videos
- listen to music
- play games

A set top box can receive television or Internet data by cable, satellite or telephone connection. It also provides two-way communication, allowing for interactive features e.g. voting or adding premium channels on a pay-per-view basis.

Television programmes can be recorded to a hard drive, allowing users to set series recordings, pause and restart programmes.

A video games console is a specialised computer system designed for playing interactive video games using a monitor, television or projector as a display.

- Most consoles allow more than one player – this is often difficult to set up on a laptop.
- Games consoles have many other uses such as browsing the web, playing DVDs and CDs, streaming movies and editing videos. Online games allow users to play against players from around the world.
- Consoles use motion sensors for hands-free gaming and allow the use of virtual reality headsets for more realistic games.

Digital cameras

Sales of digital cameras for personal use, both still and video, have tumbled since 2010.

Why have sales of digital cameras fallen since 2010?

Digital cameras store images as a collection of pixels (see Chapter 6). The more pixels in the image, the better the quality of the photo, up to a certain point. The latest mobile phone cameras take images of between 7 and 12 megapixels.

A compact camera suitable for an amateur photographer who wants a bit more control than the camera on a smartphone provides, may have manual controls over aperture, shutter speed, low light photo quality and optical zoom. With optical zoom, the camera's lens magnifies the image for much sharper results; the digital zoom feature in a cheaper camera, by contrast, enlarges the pixels in an image as the shot is taken, reducing the quality of the image. Digital Single Lens Reflex (DSLR) cameras are used by serious amateur and professional photographers.

Bluetooth connectivity on many cameras makes it easy to transfer images to another device.

Video

Many cameras also include video capability with special effects such as time-lapse and slow-motion recording. Short videos are often posted on YouTube by vloggers and other individuals, and are sometimes viewed by millions of people around the world.

Dash cams are in-car camera systems that make a video and audio recording of your journey. Many insurance policies accept dash cam evidence in the event of a car incident. If the footage proves the other party was at fault, you may not have to pay your excess, or lose any no-claims discount. As dash cams become more common, they could lower car insurance premiums, reduce theft and help deter insurance fraud.

Some dash cams include a parking mode, which starts recording whenever an impact is detected. If someone hits your car when they're parking and doesn't leave a note, there is a better chance of finding out what happened and who is responsible for the damage.

Security cameras

In 2017, more than 3.2 million British households had self-installed, connected surveillance cameras. Most security cameras now transmit live video footage to an iPhone or Android app so the home owner can tune in to see that all is safe and secure, or that the dog isn't up to no good, from wherever they are.

Security cameras are common on streets and around commercial properties, both inside and outside.

Traffic and speed cameras

Cameras are used in dozens of applications related to traffic and vehicles on the road, from self-driving trams and cars to speed cameras which capture the number-plate images of speeding vehicles. The London Congestion Charge, introduced in 2003, is based on automatic number plate recognition. The system has helped to reduce the steady increase in traffic, and the resulting congestion, on London's roads.

Navigation systems

Navigation systems are used in cars, ships and aircraft and by individuals. They may be handheld, for example on a smartphone. They can typically:

- display maps
- determine a vehicle's or person's location, their speed and the direction they are facing
- give verbal directions
- provide information on traffic conditions or obstacles and suggest alternative directions

A satellite navigation (satnav) system uses a group of satellites and computers which form the Global Positioning System (GPS) to determine the instrument's location.

Data capture and collection systems

Data capture devices include mouse, keyboard, touchscreen, barcode reader, magnetic card reader, RFID reader, biometric devices, camera, microphone, various types of sensor such as a light, temperature, moisture, pressure or movement sensor and a range of specialised devices for disabled users.

Electronic funds transfer at point of sale (EFTPOS) is an electronic payment system involving electronic funds transfers using a debit or credit card, at payment terminals located at points of sale.

Data capture devices

Some of these devices are considered in more detail in Chapters 2 and 3.

Suggest applications for magnetic card readers, RFID readers, biometric devices and sensors.

Digital technology has the potential to disrupt existing industries and create new ones. Spotify's digital streaming service has made physical media for delivering music largely irrelevant. Uber's technology connecting people who need rides with people who have cars for hire has changed the whole economy of taxi services.

Retail in successful companies is no longer just about products. It is about customers. Technology can be used to shorten or eliminate queues at the checkout, or to ensure that the shelves are stocked with products at all times, and not "out of stock". This is the least of what consumers expect of an in-store experience today.

Case Study: Amazon Go

Amazon Go is a cashier-less store wired up with cameras and sensors that track a shopper's every move. Artificial intelligence is used to recognise specific shopper behaviours. The amount of data gathered is mind-boggling. Every shopper movement, every product picked up and then dropped in a bag, every label read and product replaced on the shelf, every hesitation or head nod is recorded and analysed by the software.

 What does Amazon hope to gain by collecting all this data?

Communication devices and systems

Communication devices include network interface cards, switches, routers, and wireless access points, as well as mobile phones, Wi-Fi and Bluetooth devices.

These are all covered in chapters in Learning Aim B, Chapters 10, 12 and 13.

Exercises

1. Anna works for an advertising company. Her job is to design advertising material and source images to be used in advertisements posted on social media sites, websites and brochures. Sometimes while she is out shopping or having lunch in the park, she will see a scene that sparks her imagination.

   (a) Explain **two** features of a smartphone which she will be able to use to quickly pass on her ideas to a member of her team back in the office. [4]

   (b) Anna sometimes has to drive to meet clients in their offices. Name and describe two features of a digital device which will help her to find her way to her destination. [4]

2. Desktop and laptop computers are two common choices of device for home working.

   (a) Explain **one** advantage of a laptop over a desktop computer for someone working at home. [2]

   (b) Explain **two** advantages of a PC over a laptop for someone working in an office. [4]

   (c) Darren is a computer games player. He intends to buy a new computer.

   Describe **three** features or extra hardware devices that he should look for in the computer configuration that he purchases. [6]

3. A2B Couriers pick up and deliver parcels across the country.

   (a) Identify a device that a delivery driver may use to digitally record and store a person's signature when he delivers a parcel to them. [2]

   (b) At the end of the day the recorded signatures of all the people he has delivered parcels to are downloaded to a computer storage device at Head Office.

   Explain **two** reasons why the signature is saved on a storage device at Head Office. [4]

Chapter 2
The function and use of digital devices

Objectives

- Describe the function and use of digital devices for:
  - education and training
  - personal
  - social
  - retail
  - organisational use – business operations, internal and external dissemination of information
  - creative tasks

IT in education and training

By 2014, it was reported that, according to research, around 70% of primary and secondary schools in the UK were using tablet computers. In 9% of schools, there was an individual tablet device for every pupil. But, the study reported, *there was no clear evidence of academic improvement for pupils using tablet devices*.

On the other hand, there was some evidence that the tablets helped to motivate pupils who might otherwise be disengaged, and when pupils took the tablets home, this increased the involvement of families.

 What are the latest trends and issues in using digital technology in schools, colleges and training providers?

- Many classrooms are equipped with projectors which can be used to project the image from the teacher's computer screen. This can be used to deliver pre-prepared lessons created using PowerPoint, look at content downloaded from the Internet, or to show student presentations.

- In many classrooms, **interactive whiteboards** have largely replaced blackboards and whiteboards. They are said to increase the involvement and collaboration of the students in the classroom. The touchscreen allows a user to alter the data on their screen, or move it around, with their fingers.

- The use of mobile phones in schools has become a controversial issue.

Discuss some uses of projectors in your school or college. How useful are they?

Discuss the advantages and disadvantages of equipping classrooms with interactive whiteboards.

Case Study: "Schools should have a consistent policy on phones"

In November 2018, The Children's Commissioner for England, Anne Longfield OBE said schools across England should have a consistent approach to the use of mobile phones. She said schools could help families if they took a "bold approach".

The select committee was taking evidence about the impact of social media and screen use on young people's health. Appearing as a witness, Ms Longfield said research from her office had shown that children's social media use increased dramatically when they made the transition between primary and secondary school. Children were at 'significant' social media risk.

Ms Longfield said children spoke to her about an "avalanche of pressure", particularly in the first year of secondary school, to be popular and successful on social media.

Give arguments for and against allowing mobile phones to be used in schools.

Virtual learning environment (VLE)

- A **VLE** allows students to access their documents from home on a PC or from anywhere on a mobile device. They can view department webpages, find and use important resources for their homework or coursework and view the latest school notices.

- VLEs can be used successfully to deliver university and college courses remotely, and there are many different implementations. Thousands of students benefit each year from Open University courses. Globally, **Massive Open Online Courses** (MOOCs) can reach millions of learners.

Recommended for you

We looked through our catalogue and found a selection of courses we think you'll like:

Get your degree with us

 Follow your passion and develop high-demand skills in a variety of disciplines such as accounting and business

Specialisations

 Maths skills top-up
Keep your knowledge strong with our short or in-depth courses

Personal and social use

The personal use of a mobile phone or social media is covered in more deatil in Learning Aim C, Chapters 17 and 18.

Black box car insurance

Young drivers who have recently passed their driving test often receive an extremely high, unaffordable quote for car insurance. This is because most insurers base their premium calculations on driver profiles and statistical evidence – and, unfortunately, young and newly qualified drivers are statistically more likely to be involved in an accident than any other group.

To qualify for black box insurance, the driver's car is fitted with a small "black box" device about the size of a smartphone, which records speed, distance travelled, driving style while braking and cornering, type of road and time of day the driver most often travels, to build a comprehensive driver profile.

The driver can access a secure website to find out how they are performing in each category. This will show them if they need to make any changes to their driving style, and will provide tips on how to improve the driver score and bring down the cost of car insurance.

Case study: Road deaths fall

In November 2018 it was reported that the number of young drivers being killed or seriously injured in crashes has dropped by 35% with the increasing use of black box insurance.
There were 18,529 victims aged 17 to 19 in 2011 compared with 11,984 in 2017, according to an analysis by the Department of Transport. Four out of five young drivers are now estimated to have a black box installed in their cars, monitoring their driving habits..

Retail

Some 9,000 retail stores closed down in 2017, and the number was forecast to increase to 12,000 in 2018. The great majority of retail stores use digital technology to take cash and card payments at the till, including contactless payments. Many stores use handheld or fixed barcode scanners to scan items and adjust stock quantities. Most large supermarkets use self-service checkouts which allow the customer to scan the barcodes on products they have picked up off the shelves. These are then weighed and compared with the weight recorded on the store's computer system.

Self-service checkouts at a supermarket, and a handheld bar scanner

Barcode scanners are used in retail warehouses. Barcode technology is used to keep track of goods received or replenished and for picking, packing, shipping and returns.

A major use of digital technology in retail is concerned with gathering customer data through the use of store loyalty cards and as described in Chapter 1, tracking customer in-store behaviour.

Shoplifting costs retailers billions of pounds every year, and anti-theft devices are another use of digital technology.

Radio frequency tags used to prevent shoplifting

RFID technology can be used on expensive products. In some stores the shopper can take an item into the fitting room and RFID technology identifies the item in your hands. It then provides you with a list of the available colours and sizes on a screen, answering your question before you've even asked.

Organisational use

Organisations typically use networked PCs for business systems, accounting, management information systems and internal and external communication. Laptops and tablets may be used by employees working from home or travelling.

Learning Aims B to F give information on many aspects of organisational use of IT, and examples of its use.

Creative tasks

Computers are used in hundreds of creative tasks from creating a simple PowerPoint presentation to creating a feature-length animated film, to designing the tallest building in the world.

Case study: Manufacturing fake news

Using digital technology, a speaker's lips on a video or film can be synchronised with the words they are speaking. This revolutionary facial-mapping technology has been designed to improve television language dubbing, but it also has strong potential for those seeking to spread fake news.

It is now possible to synchronise a news-reader's facial expressions and lips with words spoken by someone else. The facial mapping technology rapidly models the details of a human face. But how can we be sure that this technology is used for its commercial benefits rather than for political disruption? In this age of information overload, it is getting harder to separate truth from fake news.

 How will anybody be able to trust what they see or hear on digital media? How can people distinguish between what is real and what is not real?

Exercises

1. CPT Training is an organisation that delivers training on software used to create self-learning packages. They have up to 12 delegates on courses given inhouse by a trainer.

    (a) Describe **two** devices and associated software they may use in the classroom for the use of the trainer and the trainees. [4]

    (b) Describe how each of these may be used. [4]

2. In2Fashion is a high-end retailer selling designer clothes online and in high street stores. They use technology to combat theft and increase sales from their high street stores.

    (a) Describe **two** ways in which technology can be used to combat theft. [6]

    (b) Describe **one** way in which the organisation may use digital devices to increase sales in their high street stores. [3]

Chapter 3
Peripheral devices and media

Objectives

Describe:

- peripheral devices used with other digital devices to form part of an IT system:
  - input devices
  - output devices
  - storage devices
- manual and automatic data processing
- accessibility devices
- characteristics and implications of storage media used to form part of an IT system

Input devices

Keyboards, mice, joysticks and touchscreens need no introduction. The uses of cameras, sensors, barcode scanners and RFID technology were discussed briefly in Chapters 1 and 2.

Barcode readers

There are two different kinds of barcode. Linear barcodes can be read using a handheld barcode scanner or a laser scanner, as for example at a supermarket checkout.

2D barcodes, such as the Quick Response (QR) code shown below, can hold more information than the linear barcode and are commonly used, for example, in ticketless entry to events. They can be read with a QR barcode reader or camera-enabled smartphone with QR reader software. A QR code is able to hold information in both the vertical and horizontal directions.

QR barcodes are also used, for example, in mobile phone apps which can take a photo of a QR code shown on a magazine advert, billboard, web page or product. This may then show you a web page address (URL) which you can click to see a movie trailer, get a money-off coupon or get more information such as a map, location or product information.

Radio Frequency Identification (RFID)

RFID tags use electromagnetic fields to automatically identify and track tags attached to objects, clothing or animals. Most RFID tags must be read within a few centimetres of the reader. Some RFID tags can be read without line of sight from up to 300 metres away, and pass information from the stored data on the tag to the receiver and vice versa.

An RFID tag is comprised of two parts: an **antenna** for transmitting and receiving signals, and an **RFID chip** (integrated circuit) which stores the tag's ID and other information.

A separate **RFID antenna** is necessary in any RFID system. This is a dumb device which uses power from the reader to transmit and receive signals from the RFID tags.

An **RFID reader** can be fixed or handheld. Most fixed readers require an Ethernet cable in order to send and receive data, while some Wi-Fi RFID readers communicate over secure wireless networks. A fixed reader typically has two, four or eight port readers to support two, four or eight antennas.

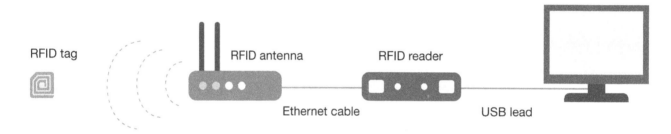

RFID tags have hundreds of different uses. For example:

- Tagging items in retail stores: The price of tags is heavily dependent on tag type and volume; the pricing on 10,000, 1,000 or 100 tags will be very different. There are many different types of tag and thorough testing will be required to ensure the system works well with the selected tag type.

- Inventory tracking:
  - Tags can be read remotely, often at a distance of several metres
  - Several tags can be read at once, enabling an entire pallet-load of products to be checked simultaneously
  - Tags can be given unique identification codes, so that individual products can be tracked

- Race timing: in marathon races, each racer has an RFID tag attached to their clothing.
- Library systems: RFID tags can be read from multiple angles making check-in and checkout of books significantly faster.

The smallest tags are about the size of a grain of rice and can be injected under the skin for the identification of a pet.

Microphone

Voice input and output is becoming increasingly common. It can be used for giving commands, for example to a car navigation system or an Amazon Echo device. The device can be trained to recognise what its owner is asking when they say any of a collection of phrases such as *"Alexa, switch on the lights!"*, *"Alexa, play 'Moonlight Sonata!'"*, *"Alexa, what's the outside temperature?"*

Amazon Echo device

Q1 **Why do you suppose devices such as the Amazon Echo often use female voices for output? Does this say anything about the perceived role of women?**

Output devices

Output devices include printers, projectors, speakers, and lights (LED devices).

Printers

Laser printers and inkjet printers are the most common types of printer used in routine office or school work, or at home. The major expense, after purchasing a printer, is the cost of the ink for an inkjet printer or toner for a laser printer.

A **3D printer** is useful for creating prototypes or one-off products.

A 3D printer

Q2 **List some specific uses of 3D printers.**

Speakers

Speakers are used to output music, beeps, alarm or warning signals and also voiced commands and explanations. Spoken text and voiced descriptions of images on screen can make a website more accessible to a blind person or someone with low vision. Voice output is useful, for example, in giving instructions to the driver using an in-car GPS navigation system.

Monitors

Some users may have multiple monitors on their desks with different orientations so that they can, for example, view a page of text in portrait view and at the same time, work on an image or search the Internet on another screen on their desk.

Manual data processing

Manual data processing typically involves entering data, processing it either manually or using software, and generating output. Processing survey results, for example, may be done partly automatically and partly manually.

Automatic data processing

Data entered by an operator responding to a telephoned order from a customer, for example, is a manual data process. However, once a telephone order has been entered, Sales Order Processing software can automatically generate all the relevant paperwork such as picking lists, delivery notes, and invoices. It can also be used to create quotes for customers, which can be turned into an order with one click.

Management information systems, which aid in decision-making and strategic planning, may produce automatically generated reports from data gathered from routine daily business transactions.

Decision-making algorithms

Thousands of decisions, from navigating self-driving cars to selecting candidates for job interviews or deciding on the length of a custodial sentence to be handed out by a judge in court, are performed entirely automatically using complex algorithms.

The videos that you are recommended on YouTube, the news that you see on Facebook, the advertisements that you see on Google and the marketing emails that you receive, are all decided automatically by algorithms, with no human intervention required.

Automated Meter Reading

Automated Meter Reading (AMR) meters accurately measure a customer's energy use and send readings directly to the energy supplier.

- For the supplier, this eliminates the need to send someone round to every customer's house to read the meter every few months.

- For the customer, it means they no longer have to read the meter themselves and send the reading to the supplier, or receive estimated bills. They receive an accurate bill every month.

- Payment may be made by **Direct Debit**, another example of automatic data processing. The correct payment is automatically taken from the customer's designated bank account with no need for any action by the customer.

 List some other examples of automatic data processing.

Accessibility devices

There are many specialised input and output devices and aids for people with a disability; for example, speech recognition software, screen readers, touch screens, specially adapted keyboards with big keys, eye motion sensors and screen magnifiers.

- A special Braille keyboard or keyboard overlay is available for blind users.

Braille keyboard

- A mouse that can be operated with a foot is available for someone who cannot use their hands.

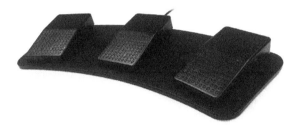

A foot mouse

- Other devices such as sip and puff devices allow quadriplegics to use a computer using only their mouth.

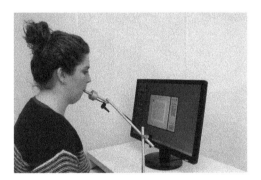

Sip and puff device

Storage devices

When choosing a storage device, the following factors may be taken into account:

- capacity
- speed
- portability
- durability
- reliability
- cost

The two types of storage available for a PC are solid state drives (SSDs) and hard disk drives. Many PCs have two drives: for example, the C: drive may be a 256Gb solid state drive (used mainly for holding software) and the D: drive a 1Tb hard drive (used mainly for holding data).

Laptop computers, especially at the high-end, are increasingly sold with an SSD. The price is now comparable with hard disk and as SSDs have no moving parts, they are more robust; rather than one or more spinning platters, an SSD consists of a collection of flash memory chips. An SSD is also much faster than a hard disk and can be made in very compact forms, leaving more space for a bigger battery. They also use less power than a hard drive and are completely silent in operation.

An SSD in a high-end laptop could typically have a capacity of 1Tb. In May 2018, Samsung unveiled an SSD with 30Tb of storage in a standard 2.5" form, but these are not yet generally available.

A hard disk and two types of SSD

Magnetic tape

Magnetic tape has traditionally been used for backups, and it is still widely used for **archiving** data. In 2018, studies showed that the amount of data being recorded is increasing at 30 to 40 percent per year. Much of the world's data, including data for basic science, radio astronomy, national archives, major motion pictures, banking, insurance, oil exploration, and more is still held on magnetic tape.

Inserting a backup tape cartridge in a data centre

A modern cartridge tape can hold 15TB of data, and although it is slow in comparison with hard disks or SSDs, it is inexpensive, extremely reliable, energy efficient and easily stored offline. It can also have built-in encryption which makes it very secure.

External hard drive

An external hard drive is a hard drive or SSD connected to the computer, typically by a USB connection. External hard drives are portable, easy to use, and can provide a large amount of storage whenever it is needed. They can be moved from computer to computer, making it easy to transfer large files and folders between computers.

External hard drives are often used to store backups.

USB flash drive

Flash drives commonly store between 16 and 512GB, with the largest-capacity devices able to store up to 1TB or more. They use very little power, have no fragile or moving parts, and are small and light. They are useful for transferring data between computers. Some flash drives have a tough rubber or metal casing which makes them waterproof and virtually unbreakable.

The disadvantage of flash drives is that they are easily misplaced or lost. Any confidential data on the drive is therefore at risk unless it has been encrypted. They can pick up a virus from an infected computer and infect any other computer that they are inserted into.

A flash drive can only be written to and erased a limited number of times before the drive fails.

SD card

An SD card is a very small flash memory card providing high-capacity storage of typically between 32 GB and 2TB. SD cards are used in many portable devices such as cameras, camcorders, audio players and mobile phones.

Optical disks

Optical disks are most often used for storing music (e.g. on a CD) or video (on a DVD or Blu-ray disk). They are often used to distribute games and other software to customers.

Exercises

1. Khalid is a blind student.

   Describe **two** accessibility devices which will help him to complete his Information Technology course and explain how each may be used. [4]

2. The Inland Revenue keeps records of tax returns made by companies and individuals for a number of years.

   (a) Discuss **two** advantages of magnetic tape over other forms of storage for archiving the data. [4]

   (b) Describe **two** other types of data which may be archived on magnetic tape. [4]

3. Passenger entry through a barrier after checking in for a flight and passing through security checks is controlled automatically, generally with no human operator intervention.

   (a) Describe **two** types of input device that could be used in this process. [4]

   (b) Describe **one** output device that could be used in this process. [2]

   (c) Explain why a human operator may also be present at the barrier. [2]

Chapter 4
Operating systems

Objectives

Describe:

- types of operating system: single-user single-task, single-user multi-tasking, multi-user, real-time
- the role of the operating system in managing: networking, security, memory, multi-tasking, device drivers

The operating system

An operating system is a program or set of programs that manages the operations of the computer for the user. It acts as a bridge between the user and the computer hardware; this is essential since a user cannot communicate with hardware directly.

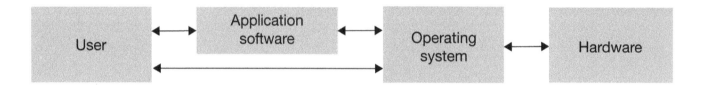

The operating system acts as a bridge between user and computer hardware

The operating system is held in permanent storage, for example on a hard disk. A small program called the **loader** is held in **ROM** (Read Only Memory). When a computer is switched on, the loader in ROM sends instructions to load the operating system by copying it from storage into **RAM** (Random Access Memory).

Functions of an operating system

Every general-purpose computing device, from a mobile phone to the largest computer server or mainframe, needs an operating system. The operating system enables the user to complete all their various tasks such as loading and running programs or apps, saving or printing files. It provides a simple **interface** to enable the user to give instructions.

Types of operating system

Single-user, single-task

In the early days of PCs, and on early mobile phones, this was the only type of operating system (OS) available. The OS could only load and run one program at a time.

By 2018, the most likely place to find such an operating system would be **embedded** in a device such as a digital camera. The OS typically has a menu interface to enable the user to select settings, and buttons and other controls to operate the camera. It is single-task in that, even though it can perform many different tasks, it cannot do more than one thing at a time.

A digital camera performs one task at a time

Single-user, multi-tasking

This is the type of operating system which runs on a standalone PC or laptop. The Windows operating system, for example, can run many jobs simultaneously, switching rapidly between them so that each one appears to be the only one running. You can, for example, be playing music, editing a Word document and checking your emails occasionally.

If you display the Task Manager by pressing **Ctrl-Shift-Esc**, you will find there are several programs in memory, most of which are not currently executing.

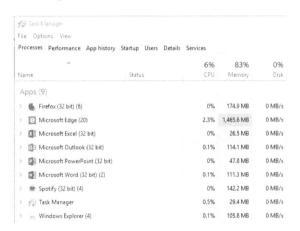

Multi-user

Time-sharing systems are multi-user, multi-tasking systems. A single powerful mainframe or supercomputer may be connected to hundreds of terminals all using the mainframe CPU. Each user gets a slice of processor time according to a **scheduling algorithm**. Very large organisations such as banks and credit card companies which process huge numbers of transactions use mainframes.

An IBM mainframe released in 2015 can process 2.5 billion transactions daily.

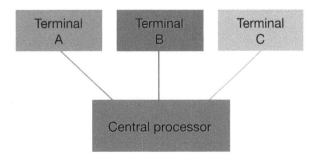

A multi-user, multi-tasking system

The role of an operating system

Managing networks

A network operating system (OS) may be based on a **client-server network** in which a **server** enables multiple **clients** to share resources. Programs and data may be held in a dedicated **file server**, enabling all client devices connected to the network to share resources as well as to save data on the server in their own user areas.

Security

The OS is responsible for the security of the network. It controls:

- **Access to a computer**, whether standalone or on a network. A user will normally have to be authenticated by typing in a password or PIN, or by using biometric identification, before they can use a computing device. On a network, depending on their user ID and password, they will only be allowed access to certain parts of the network.

- **File access.** The OS controls the file access by setting permissions to files and directories. The most common permissions are Read, Write, Delete, and Execute.

 What authentication is required when you (a) turn on your mobile phone, or (b) use a networked computer?

Memory management

A PC allows a user to be working on several tasks at the same time. You may be listening to music via a streaming site such as Spotify, entering data into a database, checking your emails every so often and running Word so that you can document your progress. Meanwhile, a virus checker may be running in the background.

Each program, open file or copied clipboard item, for example, must be allocated a specific area of memory whilst the computer is running. There are, therefore, usually many data files and programs in memory at the same time.

The allocation and management of space is controlled by the operating system. The diagram below illustrates the concept but does not show the whole picture. In reality, each program and data file is split into small, equal sized sections of typically 4K bytes called pages, which may be stored non-consecutively. The OS maintains a table of precisely where in memory each page of every file is held.

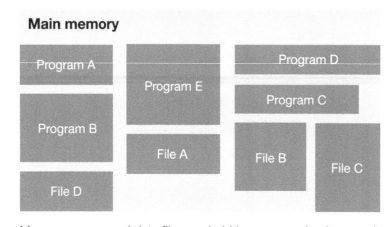

Many programs and data files are held in memory simultaneously

Virtual memory

Memory is not limitless, so as more and more jobs (called **processes**) are loaded into memory, the operating system may swap pages of temporarily inactive processes out to disk, using secondary storage as an extension of memory to make room for the next process which needs a share of processor time.

As memory fills up, you may notice a deterioration in performance as sections or **pages** of programs and data files are swapped in and out of RAM, to the point where the operating system is spending most of its time swapping pages in and out, so-called 'thrashing', and performance slows right down.

Suppose a PC that you have used for a number of years has become very slow. Suggest actions that you could take that may help to improve its speed.

Interrupts

An **interrupt** is a signal from a software program, hardware device or internal clock to the CPU. A software interrupt occurs when an application program terminates or requests certain services from the operating system. A hardware interrupt may occur, for example, when an I/O operation is complete or an error such as `Printer out of paper' occurs.

Interrupts are also triggered regularly by a timer, to indicate that it is the turn of the next process to have processor time. It is because a processor can be interrupted that multi-tasking can take place.

Managing multi-tasking

Although there may be many processes running apparently simultaneously in a computer, they are not actually running at the same time. The OS allocates each one in turn a tiny slice of processor time. If, for example, a user is writing a document and pauses to think what to write next, the OS will allocate the next task to the processor. If a long program is executing, it will only be allowed a few microseconds at a time (a time slice) before the processor is allocated to the next process.

Multiuser operating system allocates processor time to each job

Time slices

Suggest reasons why Process A only has two time slices in the above diagram.

Device drivers

A **device driver** is a computer program that provides a software interface to a particular hardware device. This enables operating systems to access hardware functions without needing to know details of the hardware being used. When you attach a new printer to your computer, for example, you will have to install the device driver program that comes with it before it will work. Sometimes the OS will do this automatically if it detects that the printer is one for which it already has a driver. Drivers are **hardware dependent** and **operating system specific**.

The device driver communicates with the device, issuing commands to carry out the required task. When a signal is received from a device, for example "out of paper" or "job complete", the device driver communicates with the OS. This causes an interrupt and the next process in the queue is allocated processor time.

Real-time operating system

A real-time operating system is used in applications that need to respond to data input within a fraction of a second.

The operating system in the flight-control system of a "fly-by-wire" airliner such as the Airbus 320 is a **real-time**, **embedded** system.

The operating system on the aircraft or similar safety-critical system must have the following features:

- It must respond very quickly to any inputs or sensors

- It must be able to deal with many inputs simultaneously

- It must have 'failsafe' mechanisms designed to detect and take appropriate action if a hardware component fails

- It must incorporate redundancy – that is, if one component fails, it must automatically switch to backup hardware

Exercises

1. Describe the following functions of an operating system.

   (a) Memory management [4]

   (b) Multi-tasking [4]

   (c) Communication with input-output devices [3]

   (d) Security [3]

2. Alan has a four-year-old PC. He thinks that it has become slow to respond to commands.

   (a) Explain **two** reasons why his PC may be operating more slowly than when it was new. [4]

   (b) Explain **two** measures that Alan could take which should improve the performance of his PC. [4]

Chapter 5
Choice and use of operating system

Objectives

- Describe factors affecting the choice and use of user interface: graphical, command line, menu based, and adaptive
- Describe factors affecting the choice of operating system
- Describe the factors affecting the use and performance of an operating system

User interface

The user interface is the way in which we interact with computer hardware. Whatever method is used for the user to communicate with a computer or computerised device, it is the operating system that provides these features.

Graphical user interface

We are all familiar with the way a PC works: clicking icons with the mouse, dragging and dropping files and folders, scrolling up and down, etc. This is a graphical user interface or GUI. It is also sometimes called a WIMP user interface. WIMP stands for Windows, Icons, Menus and Pointers. This type of interface places a much higher demand on the processor than a command line interface.

Mobile phones and tablet PCs have a slightly different user interface which allows you to move things by swiping the screen with your fingers and which can sense degrees of pressure or a change in the orientation of the device. Phones have controls that perform specific functions such as recording sound or taking a photograph.

Some computer systems are embedded in everyday machines such as cars and central heating controls. Users interact with these in different ways and the operating systems must provide appropriate user interfaces.

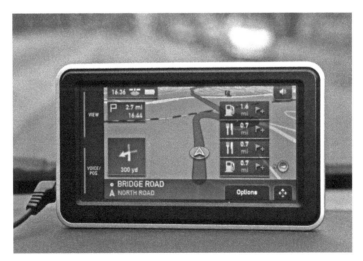

In-car satellite navigation system

What type of interface is used when setting a destination on a GPS navigation system?

Command line interface

Some computers have a **command line interface**; no mouse or menus, just a text prompt where the user types a command. Before Windows came along with its graphical user interface (GUI) in the 1980s, PCs used this type of interface. Advanced computer users sometimes prefer a simple and direct means of controlling a program or operating system, and MS Windows still provides access to a command line interface similar to MS DOS called the Command Prompt. MS DOS was largely phased out in the 1990s.

Command line interface

Menu based interface

Menu based interfaces are common in application programs, but are also used in some operating systems, typically on specialised devices. They are generally easy to use as the user does not have to memorise commands. Menus can be explored to discover the available options, and they can be made visually appealing.

However, they are less flexible than a command line interface as the user can only execute the actions that are listed. It can also be hard to find a specific menu option.

Q2   **Describe a device which has a menu-based interface.**

Adaptive interface

Most web pages and apps are now constructed so that they adapt to the size of screen being used. Whether you are using a smartphone, tablet or PC, the whole content of the web page or application will be visible.

An **adaptive** interface responds to individual users as well as to screen size. Software developers are working on interfaces that adapt to the current user. They collect data over time and anticipate each user's actions and preferences.

Voice recognition, facial recognition and other personalised functions could all be used to create adaptive interfaces.

Factors affecting the choice of user interface

In an office- or school-based environment with everyone using a desktop computer or laptop, you would expect to find almost everyone except the network manager or a few specialist programmers using a GUI. Here is a table comparing a command line interface (CLI) with a GUI.

	GUI	CLI
Ease of use	A GUI is visually intuitive and much easier to learn.	A CLI requires users to memorise commands and type them in with no errors.
Speed	Have to use a mouse and sometimes a keyboard to select files and perform other operations, which is generally slower than writing a command.	Some operations can be carried out faster using a CLI. For example, moving all files with a .jpg extension to another folder.
Memory	Requires much more memory and time to load resources such as icons and fonts, drivers for mouse and other resources such as voice input devices.	A CLI takes considerably less memory and other resources. However if the CLI is an option in Windows, nothing is saved because Windows still has to be loaded.
Multitasking	Very easy to load many different apps or files and run or vlew any of them on screen simultaneously.	Although sometimes possible, it is not easy to view multiple programs or files on screen at the same time.
New versions	New versions of a GUI, e.g. Windows 10, may mean the user has to learn new ways of doing familiar tasks.	Existing commands in a CLI rarely change, though new ones may be added.

Factors affecting the choice of operating system

Windows is overwhelmingly the most popular operating system, having a global market share of over 80%.

When we see the term "using IT systems" we tend to visualize our own experience which may well be limited to the use of a desktop PC, portable device such as a laptop or tablet, or a smartphone. On a smartphone, the choice is largely between iOS or Android. The choice of desktop computer may boil down to a choice between a Mac running a version of MacOS or a PC running Windows. If you're really adventurous or living in Italy, Cuba or some other parts of the world, you may be using a version of Linux, which is a free, open-source operating system.

A further alternative is Chrome OS, which is an online operating system. The choice of operating system may be influenced by several factors.

Security

Some operating systems have better security measures and built-in anti-virus software. Windows 10, for example, is a popular target for hackers and you are more likely to be targeted as a Windows user than as a Mac or Chrome user. However, the built-in protection software gives a good level of protection and you can install your own anti-virus software in addition.

Productivity

If the OS is already familiar to a large group of potential employees or users in the organisation, they will be able to be productive without the need for further training. Some operating systems are particularly well-suited to certain applications: for example, Macs are favoured by graphic designers. Some designers may need devices and software able to cope with CAD systems, video editing, photography projects or musical composition and may favour one operating system over another.

Other specialised users who perform specific tasks repeatedly may find a command line interface more efficient than a GUI for carrying out these tasks. Multiple commands can be saved as a script and invoked with a single command.

Cost

Some operating systems such as Linux and its variations are open source and distributed free of charge. Ubuntu is an example of an Open Source operating system and has an interface and functionality similar to Windows. Many local government organisations, home users and companies in countries such as India and Pakistan, which have many citizens skilled in computing, use Linux rather than expensive operating systems which need frequent upgrades.

Factors affecting the use and performance of an operating system

- Memory: A command line interface will occupy far less memory than a GUI.

- Suitability for the application: A special-purpose computing device such as a vehicle engine diagnostic device used by a garage may need a specialised operating system.

- Ease of use: A GUI interface may be preferable for a user who switches rapidly between applications. A command line interface may save time for an administrator or users who frequently use the same series of commands.

- Processor speed: The speed of the processor will affect performance. This may not always be significant, but a real-time operating system embedded in a car, aircraft or nuclear power station, for example, needs to react instantly to input sensors.

Exercises

1. David runs a small company which designs printed magazines and catalogues for retailers and other organisations. The company is expanding and two more designers are needed. David needs to decide what type of desktop computers to purchase for them to use in their work.

   Describe **three** factors which he should consider when choosing an operating system.   [6]

2. Alanna is the network manager in a large financial organisation.

   Describe **two** reasons why she uses a command line interface when setting network parameters or performing repetitive, frequently needed update routines.   [4]

Chapter 6
Utility and application software

Objectives

Describe:

- the purpose, features and uses of utility software

- factors affecting the choice, use and performance of utility software

- the purpose, features and uses of application software

- factors affecting the choice, use and performance of application software

- the principles and implications of open source and proprietary operating systems and software

- the impact and features of user interfaces in computer software

- the features of common file types and formats used for: images, video and application software

- the implications on IT systems, individuals and organisations of the use and selection of file types and formats

Purpose of utility software

Utility software is system software designed to optimise the performance of the computer or perform tasks such as backing up files, restoring corrupted files from backup, compressing or decompressing data, encrypting data before transmission or providing a firewall.

Features and uses of utility software

Disk defragmentation

A **disk defragmenter** is a utility program that will reorganise a hard disk so that files which have been split up into blocks and stored all over the disk will be recombined in a single series of sequential blocks. This makes reading a file quicker.

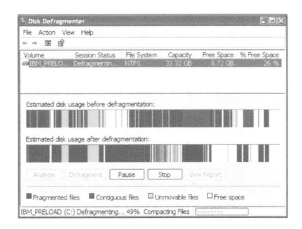

Disk defragmentation in progress

The software utility *Optimize Drives*, previously called *Disk Defragmenter*, can be set to run automatically on a weekly schedule on the latest versions of Windows. You can also optimise drives on your PC manually.

Virus checker

A **virus checker** utility checks a hard drive for viruses and removes them. Depending on the level of protection offered, incoming emails and internet downloads will also be checked and cleaned. Windows 10 comes with built-in virus protection called Windows Defender.

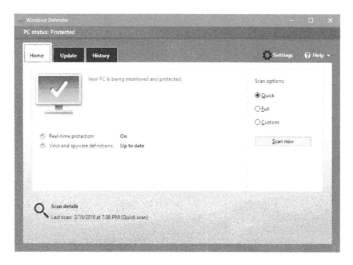

Compression software

Several utility programs are supplied as part of the operating system. These include utilities to copy, move and delete files, create, move and delete folders and to provide screensavers. Other utility programs such as WinZip for compressing and sharing files may have to be purchased from independent suppliers.

Zipped or compressed files can be transmitted much more quickly over the Internet. Sometimes there is a limit to the size of a file which can be transmitted – if you have a 15Mb photograph, you will not be able to email it to a friend if there is a 5Mb limit on the attachments they can receive. Even if they can receive the file, it may take several minutes to download if they do not have a broadband connection.

Factors affecting choice, use and performance of utility software

The factors will depend to some extent on what utility software is being sought. There are, for example, plenty of free antivirus packages.

Reading software reviews is a good start in finding the right software. The choice may depend on factors such as:

- **performance:** the software must be adequate for the task. Many utilities have a cut-down version which is free, but which does not include all the desired features or capabilities. For example, the free version of the cloud utility program WeTransfer enables users to transfer data files of up to 5GB to a remote user, but larger files can only be transferred in the paid-for version, which also offers enhanced features such as password protection. Performance of some utilities, for example those held in the cloud, or which involve storing files in the cloud, may depend on bandwidth. Some utilities may have a negative effect on the overall performance of the computer system, or conflict with other software.

- **cost:** if free software is available and does the required job, then this will be factored in to the choice. For example, Microsoft has a free inbuilt virus checker; is it necessary to pay for an additional anti-malware utility? You need to ensure that the selected utility gives excellent protection and will not adversely affect the performance of your system.

- **security:** if personal or confidential data is involved, for example, it will be important to consider security. Will data be password-protected and encrypted when using a file transfer utility, for example?

Purpose, features and uses of application software

Application software can be categorised as general purpose, special-purpose or custom-written (bespoke) software.

General-purpose software such as a word-processor, spreadsheet or graphics package, can be used for many different purposes. For example, a graphics package may be used to produce advertisements or animations, manipulate photographs or create vector and bitmapped images.

Special-purpose software performs a single specific task or set of tasks. Examples include payroll and accounts packages, hotel booking systems, fingerprint scanning systems, browser software and hundreds of other applications. Software may be bought 'off-the-shelf', ready to use, or it may be specially written by a team of programmers for a particular organisation. If, say, a hotel wants to buy some visitor booking software, they may be able to find a ready-made package that is quite suitable, or they may want a bespoke software package that will satisfy their particular requirements.

Factors affecting the choice and use of application software

Some possible criteria for selecting technology are given in Chapter 8. Many of these factors apply equally to selecting application software.

You could also consider the following:

Documentation: A well-documented package will help an individual or organisation make the most of all its facilities.

Support: Some manufacturers provide a free or paid-for support line to answer any questions regarding the software.

Training: Courses delivered either by the manufacturer or by a third party may be available for some software.

Site licensing: If multiple copies are needed, is there a good deal on a site licence?

Functionality: It is essential that the software provides all the necessary functionality.

You might consider some of the following points:

- Does it run on the available hardware?
- Is it available 'off-the-shelf' or will it have to be specially written?
- Is it well-used, tried and tested?

 What criteria would you use when deciding which word-processing software to install on your PC?

Off-the-shelf' vs bespoke software

Off-the-shelf	Bespoke software
Less expensive since the cost is shared among all the other people buying the package	More costly and requires expertise to analyse and document requirements
May contain a lot of unwanted features, and some desirable but non-essential features may be missing	Features are customised to user requirements and other features can be added as needs arise
Ready to be installed immediately	May take a long time to develop
Well documented, well-tested and error-free	May contain errors which do not surface immediately

Open source vs proprietary software

Open source software is governed by the Open Source Initiative that says:

- Software is licensed for use but there is no charge for the licence. Anyone can use it.

- Open source software must be distributed with the source code so anyone can modify it.

- Developers can sell the software they have created.

- Any new software created from open source software must also be 'open'. This means that it must be distributed or sold in a form that other people can read and also edit.

Note: This is different from **Freeware** (free software) which may be free to use but the user does not get access to the source code. Freeware usually has restrictions on its use as well.

Closed source or **proprietary software** is sold in the form of a licence to use it.

- There will be restrictions on how the software can be used, for example the licence may specify only one concurrent user, or it may permit up to say, 50 users on one site (site licence).

- The company or person who wrote the software will hold the copyright. The users will not have access to the source code and will not be allowed to modify the package and sell it to other people. This would infringe the copyright (Copyright, Designs and Patents Act 1988).

The benefit of using proprietary software is the support available from the company. There will be regular updates available and technical support lines, training courses and a large user base. Open source software tends to be more organic – it changes over time as developers modify source code and distribute new versions. There isn't a commercial organisation behind the software so there probably won't be a helpline or regular updates, just a community of enthusiastic developers.

Name an open source operating system and open source office package.

Impact and features of user interfaces in computer software

The interface can be the "make or break" issue on deciding what software to use or purchase. A good interface needs to be:

Clear: The interface must communicate the meaning and function of each option. What do the following icons communicate in the Windows 10 interface?

$$B \quad I \quad \underline{U} \; \vee \; \text{abe} \; x_2 \; x^2 \quad \underline{A} \; \vee \; \text{\small aby} \; \vee \; \underline{A} \; \vee$$

Concise: Keep explanations short. Which icon does this pop-up window clarify? What extra useful information does it give?

> **Superscript (Ctrl+Shift++)**
>
> Type very small letters just above the line of text.

Responsive: The interface should react quickly and load new options quickly. If a command starts a process which will take a long time, it should display an icon or message to the user indicating how far this operation has progressed, so the user has some idea how long they will have to wait for it to complete.

Consistent: The interface in the MS Office suite, for example, is consistent between Word, Excel and PowerPoint.

Word interface   *PowerPoint interface*   *Excel interface*

Attractive: An attractive interface can make using the software a pleasant and satisfying experience. Google, for example, changes the image on its opening screen almost daily, using topical and often amusing images.

Features of common file types and formats

Images

Images can be stored in different ways on a computer. A drawing that you create in PowerPoint is a **vector** graphic. It is made up of lines and shapes with specific properties such as line style, line colour, fill colour, start point and end point. The computer stores all this data about each shape. There are numerous different file formats for storing vector graphics. Common file extensions include .eps, .ai and .svg.

When you take a photograph on a digital camera, the image is not made up of individual shapes. The picture somehow has to capture the continuously changing set of colours and shades that make up the real-life view. To store this type of image on a computer, the image is broken down into very small elements called **pixels**. A pixel (short for picture element) is one specific colour.

The **size** or **resolution** of an image is expressed directly as the width in pixels by height in pixels, e.g. 600 x 400. If the size of a picture is increased, then more pixels will need to be stored. This increases the size of the image file. This is a **bitmap** image. The file will be stored as a collection of pixels as a **.bmp** or **.jpg** file.

100 x 67 pixels

1000 x 670 pixels

Videos

As with images, there are several different formats for video files. The AVI format, developed by Microsoft, is one of the oldest video formats. AVI files can run on a number of different operating systems like Windows, Mac and Linux, and are also supported by popular web browsers. MPEG4 is used for HTML5 videos and the files usually have the extension .mp4. They can be played on Macs, PCs and all iPhones.

File compression

Data compression techniques are covered in Learning Aim B, Chapter 13. Image and video files are commonly compressed to create smaller files. With lossy compression, unnecessary information is removed from the file. Lossless compression retains all the information so that the original file can be recreated exactly.

The following table shows some file types and file extensions for different file formats.

Type	File Extension	Compression Type	Explanation
Bitmap	.bmp	-	Uncompressed still image file
Portable Network Graphic	.png	Lossless	16.7 million different colours. Enables a transparent background
JPEG	.jpg	Lossy	Good for photographs. 16.7 million different colours
Graphics Interchange Format	.gif	Lossless	Colour depth = 8 bits (only 256 colours) Good for images with large areas of solid colour. Ideal for web graphics
MPEG 4	.mpg	Lossy	Video files: Suitable for small low-resolution sequences
MOV	.mov	Lossy	Developed by Apple for playing back movies with sound, also commonly used in Windows

Application software

Application software is executable and therefore has a .exe extension. You should always be very wary of clicking on a file with the extension .exe that you receive as an email attachment – it could be a virus, which is in effect an application program.

Implications of the use and selection of file types

Compatibility: When choosing a file type and format, compatibility with different devices needs to be taken into account. For example, a .mov video taken on an iPhone can be played on a Mac or a PC, but you may not be able to play a .mp4 file on your TV.

Portability and interoperability: Files may need to be read and interpreted by different hardware and software. For example, **PDF (Portable Document Format)** files can be read on most hardware using the free Adobe PDF viewer software.

File size: It may be inconvenient and time-consuming to transfer very large files over the Internet. A compressed file format will enable large files to be uploaded and downloaded much faster.

Future proofing: Organisations and individuals need to be sure that their files will still be readable in five or 10 years' time. Files created in different software may be unreadable if the operating system used is changed, say from a Mac to a PC, or a different word processing package is purchased, for example. Files that need to be preserved for a long time should be created using a set of formats that are likely to remain standard. For example, valuable information preserved by scientists, museums or the British Library are best stored as ASCII text files rather than in a .doc format created in a particular word processing package.

Non-proprietary, open specifications that have been openly documented by some public body (or released to them) by developers, such as .png and .jpg graphics file formats are more likely to remain readable than formats developed by leading software companies such as Microsoft. If someone with a new version of some software edits your file on their machine and sends it back to you, your older version may not be able to read it.

Exercises

1. MJB is a small business with a local area network. Every evening the network manager Malik starts the backup going, and this backs up all data on the server that has been changed since the previous backup. The data is backed up onto magnetic tape, and the tape is changed every morning. In the evening Malik takes the backup tape from the previous night home with him.

   Malik wants to change this system.
   (a) Explain an alternative method of ensuring that all data is backed up and stored off-site. [2]
   (b) Describe **two** advantages of the system you describe in part (a) over the existing system. [4]

2. Ada works for a company that produces marketing videos. She uses specialised software for this task.

   The company is considering purchasing new software for making the videos.

   Describe the factors, other than cost, that the company should consider before deciding on which software to purchase. [6]

3. Frieda is a website designer. She pays careful attention to making the user interface on each page attractive.

   Describe **three** other features of an interface to which she should pay attention. [6]

Chapter 7
Emerging technologies

Objectives

Describe:

- the concepts and implications of how emerging technologies affect the performance of IT systems
- the implications of emerging technologies on the personal use of IT systems and on the use of IT systems in organisations

Emerging technologies

Every year new devices and new ways of using information technology emerge. Technologies such as artificial intelligence, natural language processing and computer vision are evolving from being ideas on the drawing-board to technologies that are changing the way organisations work and individuals live their daily lives.

Artificial intelligence and machine learning

Artificial intelligence (AI) is the concept of machines being able to carry out tasks in a way that we would consider 'intelligent'.

Machine learning is based on the idea that we should be able to give machines access to data and let them learn for themselves. The more data a machine sees, the more 'intelligent' it will become. While it is being 'trained', for example to control a driverless car, it is constantly being corrected by the human trainer if it makes a wrong decision, while correct decisions are reinforced.

Driverless cars

There are **moral and ethical implications** involved in the algorithms which control a driverless car. The prospect of large numbers of self-driving cars, trucks and buses on our roads raises ethical questions about the morality of different algorithms which could be used in the face of causing 'unavoidable harm'. Who gets harmed and who gets spared?

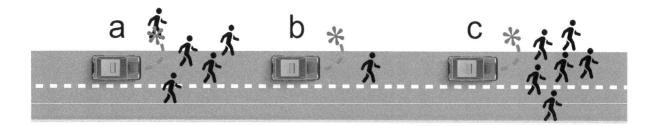

(a) The car can stay on course and kill several pedestrians, or swerve and kill one passer-by

(b) The car can stay on course and kill one pedestrian, or swerve and kill its passenger

(c) The car can stay on course and kill several pedestrians, or swerve and kill its passenger

The MIT Technology Review asked: "*Should different decisions be made when children are on board, since they have a longer time ahead of them than adults, and had less say in being in the car in the first place? If a manufacturer offers different versions of its moral algorithm, and a buyer knowingly chose one of them, is the buyer to blame for the harmful consequences of the algorithm's decisions?*"

Artificial intelligence in medicine

Computers are being trained in the art of **medical diagnosis**. Here is a simplified explanation of this process.

The computer is 'trained' by giving it millions of scans, each with a confirmed diagnosis. When the computer is presented with a scan that it has not seen before, it has been shown that it is, on average, more accurate than a human doctor in detecting and diagnosing an abnormality. The more data the computer has, the more reliable its diagnoses become.

AI has the potential to revolutionise health care. Computers, which can diagnose medical conditions or diseases at least as accurately, if not better than a human doctor, could relieve pressure on the NHS. It could bring health care to parts of the world where doctors are scarce.

Babylon Health is an example of a company providing health services, though not a diagnosis, using AI.

 What are the implications of using computer-aided diagnosis in the UK for (a) the NHS and (b) the patients?

"The computer will see you now."

Emerging technology in retail

Fifty years ago, a local shopkeeper would make sure that the right amount of stock was on the shelves by doing a visual check. A friendly face-to-face service helped to keep customers loyal. Now, it's not the local supermarket, but the online retailers who know who you are, with personal information on your name and credit card details, where you live, what you have bought in the past, how much you regularly spend and what new products are likely to appeal.

As more and more people do their shopping online, it becomes more difficult for retailers to justify spending huge amounts on opening new stores. They have to find new ways of improving the customer experience to keep their existing customers loyal.

Case study: Tesco's "Scan Pay Go" technology

In 2018 Tesco started trialling new 'shop and go' technology that allows customers to scan and pay for their groceries on their smartphone as they pick items off the shelves, then walk out of the store without visiting a till.

 Can this work? How do you pay for six carrots? What will stop people simply walking out without paying? What are the implications of this emerging technology for the millions of retail jobs, if checkouts start to disappear throughout the country?

Emerging technology in education

The traditional classroom, with a teacher standing at the front and scribbling on the blackboard or whiteboard while students take notes, is changing. The vast majority of students today could be described as 'digital natives'; completely familiar and comfortable with the use of technology, in or out of the classroom. Virtual reality headsets are also emerging as potentially game-changing ways to engage and teach students of any age. Imagine being 'present' at the Battle Hastings or following a blood platelet around the heart.

The use of technology can encourage active, collaborative, problem-based learning. It can give students better feedback and produce better results.

Using a PC, laptop, tablet or smartphone, a student can, for example:

- access the internet
- annotate an online textbook
- take a photograph of what is on a whiteboard or PowerPoint display instead of struggling to take notes

Using a Learning management system (LMS) or Virtual Learning Environment (VLE), the teacher can:

- distribute content
- collect work and assign grades
- communicate with students
- assess students and evaluate the success of the course

 What are the barriers to be overcome before schools adopt a new Learning Management System?

Wearable devices

The wearable technology market has grown exponentially over the past few years. Fitness trackers incorporating Bluetooth LE radio, an accelerometer, and heart rate and temperature sensors are readily available built in to a stylish-looking watch or piece of jewellery.

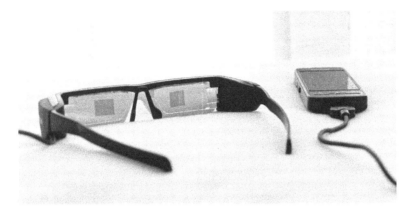

Spectacles are one form of wearable technology

A pair of glasses costing around £1,000 will enable you to see overlaid information such as patient data, mapping directions, restaurant menus, weather information, alerts, social media posts and more, by simply touching the touchpad or display button built into the frame. There's no longer any need to look at your smartphone to keep in touch with your friends!

Information displayed by the smart spectacles

New developments in data storage

Moore's Law, based on observation, stated in around 1970 that the number of transistors on an integrated circuit board would double about every two years. For decades this held true. CPU speed, size or storage capacity doubled, while prices continued to fall.

By 2018, however, new innovations were needed, and the concept of **DNA storage** emerged. In nature, DNA molecules contain genetic blueprints for living cells and organisms. Researchers at the European Molecular Biology Laboratory (EMBL) have encoded audio, image, and text files into a synthesized DNA molecule about the size of a dust grain, and then successfully read the information from the DNA to recover the files, claiming 99.99% accuracy. Professor Sriram Kosuri, a scientist at Harvard, believes that all the digital information currently existing in the world could reside in four grams of synthesized DNA.

What are the possible implications of this technology for organisations currently holding massive amounts of data in data centres around the world?

The implications of adopting an emerging technology

Being at the forefront in adopting a new technology is not usually the safest place to be. For an individual, it may be a waste of money when something better comes along within a short space of time. For an organisation, technology that is not tried and tested may mean problems with compatibility, a need for extensive staff training, and disgruntled customers if it fails to work as expected. On the other hand, it may give a company a competitive advantage.

Risk management

Cloud computing, Bluetooth technology, connected devices, robotics and artificial intelligence have all been available for some time but could still be classified as emerging technologies. Adopting them to improve the customer experience and increase efficiency may be necessary for an organisation's success and survival.

However, there are risks attached to adopting new technology too quickly. Careful planning, risk management and leadership from the top of the company are essential when introducing new technologies.

New security risks need to be analysed. For example, mobile devices brought in from outside the organisation present a new security threat. Malware could be introduced into a company network, or information could be stolen.

Hiring and training

Making major changes to how a company operates on a day-to-day basis will mean employees need to be trained. New employees with a knowledge of the new technology may need to be hired, and may be difficult to find.

Exercises

1. Basil owns a small building company, employing six people and attracting customers wanting to build an extension or have work done on their home. He has been slow to adopt new technology, and does not yet have a website. Invoicing customers is done manually, but he does have a computer for accounting purposes.

   (a) Describe **two** reasons why Basil may be unwilling to embrace new technology. [4]

   (b) Describe **two** possible benefits to Basil of having a website constructed and embracing new technology in his business. [4]

2. A **chatbot** is a piece of automated messaging software that uses AI to converse with people. Bots are programmed to understand questions, provide answers, and execute tasks.

   NewAge Software has developed a popular business software package which has been adopted by many organisations. NewAge receives many telephone calls to its helpline asking how to perform various tasks with the software, and at busy periods callers have to wait a long time for a response.

   The manager is planning to introduce chatbots to answer common queries.

   Discuss the potential benefits and drawbacks to NewAge of introducing this new technology. [6]

Chapter 8
Choosing IT systems

Objectives

- Describe the factors affecting the choice of digital technology:
  - User experience – ease of use, performance, availability, accessibility
  - User needs, specifications, compatibility, connectivity, cost and efficiency
  - Implementation – timescales, testing, migration to new system(s)
  - Productivity, security

The choice of digital technology

For an organisation, the choice of hardware and software is rarely simple. There are many factors to be taken into consideration and the choice may be a compromise between a bold leap into the unknown, and the choice of a tried and tested system. They may have to choose between an expensive system that will fulfil their projected needs for years to come, and a less expensive option that will perform all of the essential functions but may need to be changed again in the short to medium term.

The choice will be based on many different and sometimes conflicting factors. These factors will depend to a large extent on the particular software or IT system being replaced or installed for the first time. There is a big difference between choosing a new smartphone and replacing an online sales ordering system in a global retailing company!

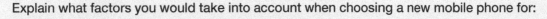

Explain what factors you would take into account when choosing a new mobile phone for:

(a) yourself

(b) an elderly relative who has never owned one before

(c) someone with an extreme need for privacy, designed for temporary use and then discarded (e.g. a 'burner' phone)

User experience

- **Ease of use:** How technologically confident are the people who will be using the system? A sales and accounting system which will be used throughout a company for different purposes needs to be easy to use, since there may be a fairly high staff turnover and new staff need to quickly get up to speed.

- **Performance:** A system needs to be fast and reliable. A user on a website, for example, may be put off by "Please wait" messages. How robust is the system? Will it detect invalid entries and display meaningful error messages?

- **Availability:** Customers using an online system to place orders or use a service may expect the service to be available 24 hours a day, especially if it operates globally over different time zones.

- **Accessibility:** Websites and commercial systems need to be made accessible for users with a disability. For example, partially-sighted users may need text to be spoken and images to be verbally described.

User needs

A graphic designer or a lab technician, for example, will have quite different needs from an accountant, commercial director or production controller. Does the system produce the required reports in a suitable format? Is specialised hardware needed for a designer or lab technician?

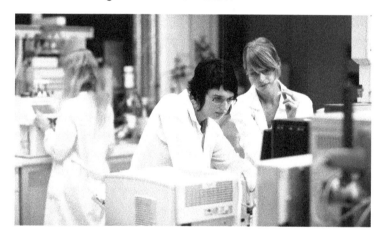

Specifications

A very clear understanding of what the system is required to do, and the problems it is designed to solve, is needed. Different tasks may need different types of device, different amounts of RAM, more powerful processors. It is also usually necessary to consider scalability – are current volumes of data expected to increase in the next few years?

Compatibility

If new technology is to be installed, compatibility with an older system is an important consideration. An incompatible system will often mean extensive staff retraining and extra cost. Compatibility of devices is also an issue – for example a decision may be made that all members should use an iOS phone so that they can use Facetime.

Connectivity

A good broadband connection is essential in many circumstances, and this may have to be installed. A company network will need to be designed with user needs in mind. Some employees may work from home or while travelling and a VPN may need to be used for security purposes (See Learning Aim B, Chapters 11 and 12.)

Cost

It is the value, rather than the cost, of a system that needs to be understood and considered. A very expensive management information system may pay for itself in a relatively short time by enabling the management to gain a better understanding of their customers' needs and make better business decisions.

Efficiency

How quickly can the users perform frequently needed tasks? Will it be more efficient to use a command line interface rather than a GUI? If a GUI is used, does the software provide shortcuts, quick keys or the ability to write and use macros for common tasks?

Implementation

- **Timescales:** How long will it take to install the new system? What staff training will be needed?

- **Testing:** How much testing needs to be done, and who will do the testing? If this is a specially commissioned system, extensive in-house testing will be needed before the system goes live.

- **Migration to new system(s):** This may be complex. It may require the old system and the new system to be run in parallel while testing is in progress. Data files may need to be in a different format, with different information, on a new system. Some historical data on customer purchases could be lost.

- **Disposal of old devices:** Obsolete hardware should be recycled, for environmental reasons. If storage devices are being replaced, all data should be wiped and disks reformatted to ensure that personal data is protected and confidential information is not seen by anyone else.

Productivity

The new system should enable staff to be as productive as possible. Data entry should be fast and easy, procedures memorable and shortcuts provided where they are useful. When a user gets 'stuck' or can't figure out how to perform a particular task, is there a helpline to the vendor?

Security

Many companies install dozens of new applications every year. Even medium-size organizations typically own several hundred applications, and large companies may have upwards of 10,000. Often, they are not aware that they are vulnerable to security threats.

Many of these applications may be held in the cloud, with more than one cloud provider involved. But in general, cloud providers do not secure the applications for users, making it clear that securing customer applications is a shared responsibility.

- A small company with only a few applications may be able to choose applications that have built-in security.

- Larger companies with hundreds of applications need a centralised management system to ensure that each application adheres to company policies and processes. Such a system should reduce risk while improving overall security and performance.

Case Studies

Every case will be different, and every case will require different factors to be taken into account. The examples which follow are designed to help you answer questions on this topic.

For each case study, go through the list of factors listed in this chapter. You would do well to memorise this list. Which factors are relevant in the given scenario? For every two marks allocated to the question, you need **one** factor with an explanation of **why** it is important. Try and answer the questions before turning to the end of the chapter for a possible answer.

Example 1

A 2018 study in the US found that serious, non-fatal workplace injuries in the US resulted in $60 billion being paid out in workers compensation costs.

A large construction company is planning to use technology to improve the safety of workers. They are focussing on:

- **Purchasing new hardware to protect workers from danger.** They are considering equipping each construction worker with smartboots that will issue automatic alerts for unsafe environmental conditions and hazards using sensors that can detect temperature, motion and location.

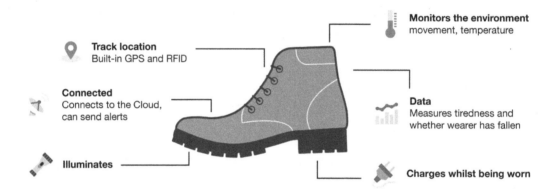

Wearable technology for construction workers

The company is also considering introducing drones to limit the amount of work that their employees have to do in unsafe areas.

- **Using software to anticipate and avoid danger.** Construction management software will gather data from wearables and drones, including data on worker fatigue throughout the day and in certain areas, as well as inspection reports from drones that highlight unsafe areas on the job site.

Discuss the factors that the company should consider before introducing these measures. (8 marks)

Example 2

Greg's is a rapidly growing business. They manufacture many kinds of wearable technology, including smartboots for the construction industry, and a smartshoe designed for use by athletes to collect physiological and biomechanical data to build a personalised running plan to optimise an athlete's form.

The managing director is planning to buy a **customer relationship management** (**CRM**) system to get a comprehensive overview of the current, past and future demand for their products.

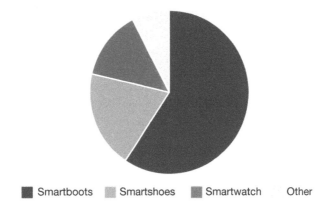

■ Smartboots ■ Smartshoes ■ Smartwatch Other

A CRM analyses sales data

Discuss factors, apart from cost, that the company should consider before deciding on a system to purchase. (8 marks)

Example 3

Helen runs a horse riding stables. She is thinking of introducing an online booking system for riders to book sessions.

Discuss the factors, apart from cost, that Helen needs to consider when creating the online system. (8 marks)

Answering case study sample questions

Step 1: From the list of possible factors, write down all those which you consider are relevant. For example, looking at the first case study given in Example 1, ease of use, performance, user needs, specification, connectivity and cost could all be considered relevant.

Step 2: Select the most obvious one first and think carefully about why you have chosen it. Make sure you can explain or justify it in a way that will earn you a mark.

Step 3. Repeat for three more factors. Don't waffle, use good English, include key words such as performance, accessibility, connectivity and technical terms where relevant. Organise your points in a coherent, logical sequence.

Example 1 Answers

The company should consider the **cost** of purchasing smartboots and the software system for gathering the data and reporting on it. The cost needs to be weighed against the possibly massive costs of paying out compensation to injured workers, or high insurance premiums for insuring against these risks.

Connectivity could be an issue. The alerts and other data will be sent wirelessly to the Head Office where the data will be monitored and analysed. There could be areas on site or in certain parts of the country where the construction company operates, where a Wi-Fi signal is not available.

Performance will be important for both the boots and the drones. The boots will need to be robust and not easily damaged. They will also need to be comfortable for the construction workers to wear.

User needs in terms of the reports that are output by the system must be carefully considered. The company needs to consider carefully what information they need in order to ensure the highest possible level of safety for all workers. They must ensure that the reports will provide them with this information.

Example 2 Answers

The company needs to consider the **specifications** of the new system. They need to write a list of all the information that they need for the system and ensure that it will be provided. They also need to consider the volume of data the system will handle and whether it is scalable, when the company expands.

Implementation needs to be considered. The amount of time that testing and implementation will take, and how much training will be required are a consideration.

Accessibility may be an issue if the company has a disabled employee or may hire one in the future. A special interface may be required.

The management needs to ensure that **productivity** will be improved by the use of the new system. It should be quick and easy to get the information that an employee needs.

Example 3 Answers

User needs and **ease of use** are important. Helen should consider whether people booking a ride will find the system useful and user-friendly. She should also consider **accessibility** if she caters for disabled riders who may want to use the system to book a session.

The **efficiency** of the system for Helen will be a factor in her decision. Since Helen will use it most of the time, it needs shortcuts and quick ways of checking bookings and responding to queries. It will mean that she will rarely need to take phone bookings which may be inconvenient if she is taking a ride, but she may want to respond to a query using a smartphone.

Exercises

1. Vikram owns a small newsagents and general store. He employs boys and girls to deliver newspapers and magazines to his customers every day. He is considering upgrading his software in order to keep more accurate records of what newspapers have to be delivered each day, how much each customer owes at the end of the month and when they last paid.

    Discuss the factors, apart from cost, that Vikram should consider before upgrading to new software. [8]

2. A school is considering purchasing new software for timetabling classes and teachers.

    Discuss the factors that the school management should consider before upgrading to new software. [8]

Transmitting data

In this section:

Chapter 9
Connectivity

Objectives

- Explain wireless and wired methods of connecting devices and transmitting data within and between IT systems

- Discuss how the features of connection types can meet the needs of individuals and organisations

(Note: Other specification points in B1 are covered in the next chapter.)

Connecting devices

Computing devices within an organisation such as a school or business need to be able to communicate:

- with each other

- with shared devices such as printers and scanners

- with the Internet

In order to enable this communication, computers are connected to form a **local area network (LAN)**. This consists of a collection of connected computers and peripheral devices (such as printers). A LAN covers a small geographical area such as one building or single site. It is normally owned by a single person or organisation.

Connection to the Internet is normally provided by an **Internet Service Provider (ISP)**. An ISP is a company that provides individuals and other organisations with access to the Internet and other related services.

Network interface

Every computer attached to a network must have an electronic circuit called a **network interface controller (NIC)**, also known as a **network interface card** or **network adapter**. In modern PCs and laptops the network interface is built into the motherboard so a separate network interface card is not required.

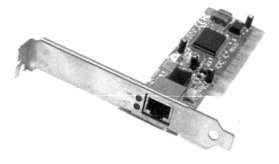

Network interface card

The network interface often has an external jack into which you can plug a network cable.

Devices may be connected either by means of cables, or wirelessly.

Wired connections

Copper cables

Cables may be made either from copper or glass (fibre-optic cable). Copper cable used in networks usually comes in the form of **twisted pair cable**. This consists of several pairs of insulated copper wire twisted around each other, each pair having one wire sheathed in a solid colour, the other striped.

The maximum length of a single run of cable is 100 metres. There are different types of twisted pair network cable, with newer types still in development.

Types of twisted pair cable

- **Cat 5e** cable (which has replaced Cat 5 cable) has four data pairs and is able to carry network data at speeds up to 1 Gbps. It is sometimes referred to as Gigabit Ethernet cable. This is the least expensive option for wiring a network.

- The newer and more expensive **Cat 6** cable can carry data at up to 10 Gbps. When transmitting 10Gbps speeds, the maximum length of a single run is only 37-55 metres.

- **Cat 6a** can support 10 Gigabit Ethernet at 100 meters. It has stronger sheathing which makes it thicker than Cat 6 and less flexible to work with. It is better suited for industrial environments where unsightly cabling is not a significant issue. The stronger sheathing eliminates **crosstalk** (interference from adjacent wires).

Even though Cat 6 and Cat 6a cabling offer higher performance rates, many LANs still opt for CAT 5e owing to its cost-effectiveness and ability to support Gigabit speeds.

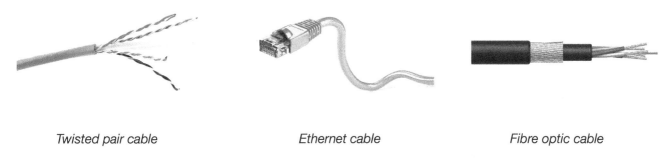

| *Twisted pair cable* | *Ethernet cable* | *Fibre optic cable* |

Ethernet connectivity

Ethernet is the standard technology for connecting wired LANs. Ethernet is the name of a low-level network **protocol**, or set of rules, describing how network devices format and transmit data packets across networks. These rules are rigidly defined to specify the electrical characteristics of the hardware used by most LANs. The connecting twisted pair cable is often referred to as an **ethernet cable**.

Protocols are explained further in Chapter 13.

Fibre-optic cable

Fibre-optic cable is made from glass that becomes flexible when it is thin. Digital information travels along fibre-optic cables as **light signals** or photons at close to the speed of light, about 30 times faster than electrons travelling along copper cables. It has a maximum run length of up to 2 km.

Network hardware

Network switch

Computers in a LAN connected by either copper or fibre-optic cable need one or more **switches** to connect all the computers to each other. Data is sent between computers and to and from the router in units called **packets**. Each packet contains a packet number, the address of the source and destination computers and typically up to 1000 or 1500 (the maximum for Ethernet) bytes of data. The switch examines each data packet and routes it to the correct computer in the network.

Network router

A router is used to connect two networks – typically, to connect the LAN to the Internet. The router is connected to the switch and also to the Internet via an **Internet Service Provider** (ISP). In small networks, the switch and the router are combined in a single device.

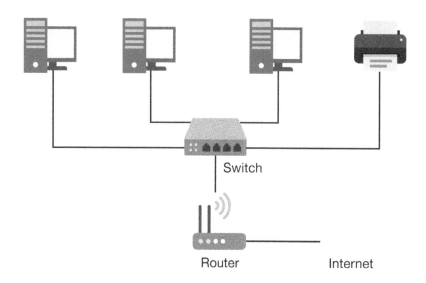

Switch

Router   Internet

A local area network with separate switch and router

Large wired networks

A large network with several hundred computers may have several switches connected by cable, known as a **backbone**. In some networks, the backbone may use fibre-optic cable, and the devices connected to a switch use copper Cat 5 or Cat 6 ethernet cable.

The ethernet handoff shown in the diagram opposite is the connection supplied by the ISP; in this example it has an ethernet interface. It establishes the demarcation point – the ISP is responsible for everything between this point and the Internet, and the customer for everything on the private side of the network.

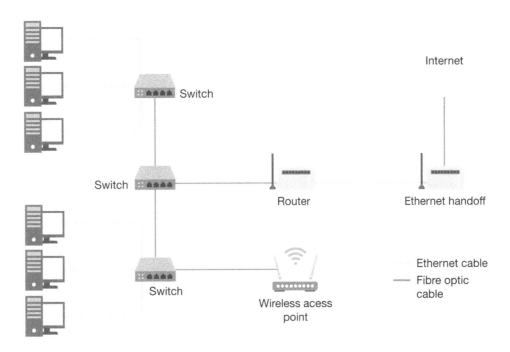

Larger network with switches and fibre backbone

Give reasons why the switches may be connected with fibre-optic cable rather than Ethernet cable.

Wireless connections

In a **wireless network** (WLAN), the computers use **wireless network adaptors** that communicate via radio signals using **Wi-Fi**. The range is typically 50 metres or less. All modern laptop computers, smartphones and most desktop computers, have built-in wireless network adapters. A Wi-Fi network can be configured in two different ways:

- "Ad hoc" mode allows wireless devices to communicate in peer-to-peer mode with each other. (See Chapter 11.)

- "Infrastructure" mode allows wireless devices to communicate with a central node that in turn can communicate with wired nodes on the LAN.

A home network or a very small business network may use a composite device that typically incorporates several distinct components including:

- a **router**, used to connect the LAN to the Internet Service Provider's network

- a **switch** with between 8 and 16 ports to connect wired devices such as computers and printers

- a **wireless access point (WAP or AP)** to connect wireless devices such as smartphones and laptops

- a **firewall** to provide protection against hackers

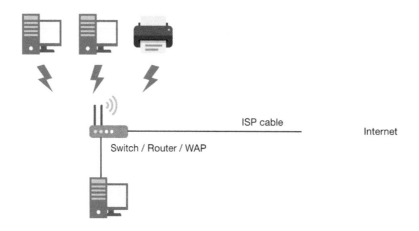

Wireless network

Wireless access points are commonly used in large office buildings to create a single wireless local area network (WLAN). Each access point may be able to support up to 255 client computers. By connecting access points to each other, local area networks having thousands of access points can be created. Client computers may move between each of these access points as needed.

Bluetooth is a wireless technology standard for exchanging data over short distances using short-wavelength UHF radio waves. It allows any two enabled devices such as smartphones and laptops to communicate or transfer files. Bluetooth can be used to link peripheral devices to a computer. Bluetooth has a minimum range of 10 metres, and can be as much as 1km.

Applications include:

- communication between a smartphone and a handsfree headset
- wireless communication between a PC and input or output devices such as mouse and printer
- transfer of documents, photos, videos, contact details, calendar appointments between devices

Connecting to the Internet

The router connects directly to a phone line via an **ethernet handoff** or a **cable modem** provided by the Internet Service Provider (ISP)/carrier to enable your computer to communicate with the ISP over a landline connection. It is also possible to connect to the Internet using 3G or 4G data over the mobile network.

In order to get superfast broadband, fibre-optic cable must be laid. About 90% of the UK can receive superfast broadband, with maximum speeds averaging over 70 Megabits per second (Mbps).

Bandwidth and broadband

Bandwidth is the range of frequencies that a transmission medium can carry. The larger the range, the greater the amount of data that can be carried in a fixed amount of time. Think of a pipe carrying water; the greater the width of the pipe, the more water that can flow along it per second.

Broadband is a high-speed connection to the Internet. The wide range of frequencies allows multiple data users as well as traditional television channels to use the same cable.

(*Note: Cable television, provided by Virgin Media and BT, is a system of delivering TV programmes to consumers via radio frequency (RF) signals transmitted through coaxial or fibre-optic cables. Satellite TV, such as Sky, uses a communications satellite to transmit TV signals.*)

Explain what happens to transmission speed when many users are downloading multimedia files simultaneously.

Sometimes small private companies lay fibre-optic cable in rural areas to provide superfast broadband.

Tove Valley Broadband is an example of a not-for profit company that engaged an installation company to lay fibre-optic cable in Northamptonshire.

Laying broadband cable in Tove Valley

Exercises

1. (a) Describe what is meant by **Bluetooth** technology.   [4]

    (b) Describe **two** applications of Bluetooth technology.   [4]

2. Four computers are to be connected in a small local area network.

    (a) Describe **three** methods which could be used to connect the computers.   [6]

    (b) State **two** hardware devices that would be needed to enable the computers in the network to access the Internet.   [2]

    (c) Draw a labelled diagram, showing devices and connections, of a small network to which different computing devices can be attached.   [4]

B

Chapter 10
Implications and impact of connection types

Objectives

- Examine the implications of selecting and using different connection types
- Evaluate the impact of connection types on the performance of an IT system

Wired or wireless: the implications

The cables or wires connecting devices in a wired network enable increased security, reliability, control and speed. Wireless connections offer flexibility.

Security

With a wired network, an intruder must first gain access to the building to physically connect to the network. Once inside the building, he or she requires physical access to a network jack or cable.

Accessing a wireless network does not require physical access. If someone is within range of a network's radio signals, they may be able to gain access to the network. For example, in a multi-storey office building, someone on the floor above or below may be in range. The lobby, car park or nearby roads may also be in range.

Wireless networks support strong encryption using Wi-Fi Protected Access (WPA/WPA2). Installing WPA2 security on a network will ensure secure connectivity between wireless systems and a corporate network. However, if employees are allowed into the wireless network using their own personal devices, the system becomes vulnerable to hacking and viruses.

If the data held on the network is particularly sensitive or confidential, a wired network will be a better choice.

Reliability

Wired connections are more consistent than wireless connections. In a home network, wireless signals are subject to interference from other home appliances including microwave ovens, cordless phones and garage door openers.

In a corporate network, an unstable wireless connection can have a detrimental effect on software performance, and productivity will suffer.

Control

With a cabled network, unauthorised users cannot use the network, using up bandwidth and slowing down the network with non-essential traffic. Tablets and smartphones also use bandwidth and may affect performance.

Freeloaders are intruders who gain access to a network and use it rather than paying for their own broadband connection to the Internet, or for performing illegal activities that cannot be traced back to them. To prevent hackers from gaining unauthorised access to a network, the network manager should ensure that network encryption is properly configured for WPA or WPA2.

New routers may be installed with the default username *admin* and a blank password. It is essential to set a strong password of at least eight characters which does not use complete words and uses a combination of character types.

Speed

Wired connections are faster than wireless connections.

A wireless network requires a central device called the wireless access point (WAP), which needs to be installed in a central location so that radio signals can reach it with minimum interference. A wireless router combines a router and a WAP. Wi-Fi performance degrades on computers further away from the Wireless Access Point (WAP). Extra routers and/or WAPs may need to be installed to ensure that productivity is not affected.

In the open, Wi-Fi signals can reach 30 metres or more but walls and other obstructions will reduce their range.

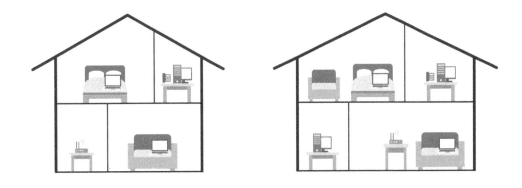

Placement of a router in a home network affects Wi-Fi signal

Many wireless routers and wireless access points can theoretically support up to 250 connected devices. The speed rating of access points represents the maximum theoretical bandwidth they can support. However, bandwidth is shared between all the users currently using the network connection, so a Wi-Fi router rated at 300Mbps with 100 devices connected only offers an average of 3Mbps to each device.

- In a home network with all devices sharing a single Internet connection, performance will start to degrade as more devices start using the network simultaneously. If one person is downloading large files or streaming a film, other users will find their connection slows down considerably.

- Access points overheat and stop working if they are overloaded.

- Several Wi-Fi clients located close together will cause radio interference, which will degrade performance and eventually cause the connection to drop.

Improving performance on a home installation

- Installing a second router or access point helps distribute the network load and will improve performance for all users.

- It may be possible to pay an increased monthly broadband subscription and get increased bandwidth.

Flexibility

The main advantage of wireless connections is ease of installation and flexibility. There are no cables to be run through walls or ceilings, and client computers on the LAN may be located anywhere within range of the nearest wireless access point. This makes it much easier to install new devices such as games consoles, printers or scanners as well as desktop computers.

It can be time-consuming and difficult to lay cables through walls or under floors when computers are in different rooms. Some newer office buildings and homes are pre-wired with Cat 5 cable, which obviously simplifies the installation process.

 Q1 **Describe the advantages of a wired rather than a wireless connection in a home network.**

Copper vs fibre-optic

When several computing devices are joined in a local area network, they can be connected either **wirelessly** or by **cable**, which may be **copper** (twisted pair) cable or **fibre-optic**.
The choice between ethernet or fibre-optic cable depends on factors such as **performance**, **cost**, **security**, and **ease of installation**.

Performance

- Fibre-optic cable is immune to electro-magnetic interference, which may be important on a factory floor or in dangerous environments such as chemical plants where a spark could trigger an explosion. Unlike copper cabling, it is not a fire hazard as it is non-flammable. Since no electricity runs through it, it does not overheat.

- Industrial plants often need fast, high-quality connections to connect control systems to their networks.

- Cat 5 and Cat 6a copper cabling have a distance limit of about 100m, including running up and down walls, compared with up to 2km for fibre-optic cable. For this reason, fibre-optic cabling may be used as the backbone connecting routers and switches in a local area network covering a large building or site.

- Speed depends on many factors but in general fibre-optic offers faster transmission speed.

Cost

Ethernet cables and switches are initially less expensive, but the relative ease of installation, higher speeds and long-distance capabilities of fibre-optic cable make it very cost effective. A telephone conversation costs about one percent as much on fibre-optic cable as it does on copper cable.

Security and reliability

Because the light signals are not subject to electro-magnetic interference, fibre-optic connections are extremely reliable; a signal can only be interrupted by someone physically cutting the cable.

Ease of installation

Any "kinking" during installation of Cat 5 cables will have a detrimental effect on performance. Fibre-optic cable is lightweight, smaller in diameter, much stronger, and is less liable to kink.

Cellular connections

There are usually two ways to connect a mobile phone to the Internet – through the cellular telephone service provider or by using standard Wi-Fi.
A Wi-Fi enabled device enables the user to access the Internet at free Wi-Fi hotspots in hotels, airports, cafes, libraries and many other locations. This is an advantage if the phone network connection is weak. A further advantage of using Wi-Fi is that data downloaded does not count in a monthly data allowance.

Using a cellular telephone service provider, the phone connects to the Internet with a wireless link in the same way that a PC does. **5G** phones will soon replace **4G** phones, giving improved speed, coverage and reliability.

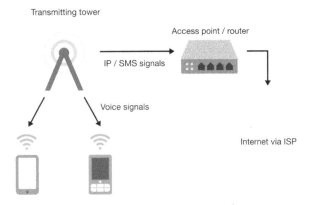

Accessing the Internet from a mobile phone

A cellular network is a cluster of geographic locations each known as a cell, which connect to the Internet through satellites. Each cell has at least one base transceiver station (transmitting tower). Mobile phones connect to a cell tower in the area, and instead of connecting to another phone it connects to the Internet and can fetch or retrieve data.

In good conditions, the signal can reach about 22 miles. However, since radio signals travel in straight lines, the signal may be blocked if the phone does not have a sight line to the tower. Towers are usually located on the highest ground possible so as to maximise the signal range.

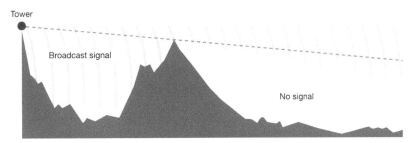

Mobile signal blocked

In towns, small antennae are placed around the city. Radio waves bounce and deflect off buildings, and finding a good signal is less of a problem. Wired glass windows, chain link fences and chicken wire may completely block a signal.

Inside a building, roofs, walls, floors, ceilings, windows, furniture and kitchen appliances all reduce a signal. You may find, for example, you get a better signal upstairs near an open window.

Exercises

1. (a) Explain **two** security vulnerabilities of a wireless network. [4]

    (b) Describe **two** advantages of a wireless, rather than a wired, local area network. [4]

    (c) Describe **two** advantages and **one** disadvantage of fibre-optic cable over copper cable. [6]

2. Anna has recently moved to a rural location in the Midlands. She has not been able to find employment, so she is thinking of setting up a small business buying and selling goods on eBay.

    She plans to install a home network connected to the Internet.

    Discuss the factors relevant to connectivity that she will need to consider when setting up her network. [8]

Chapter 11
Types of network

Objectives

- Describe the features, use and purpose of different networks:
  - Personal area network (PAN)
  - Local area network (LAN)
  - Wide area network (WAN)
  - Virtual private network (VPN)
- Describe the concepts and implications for individuals and organisations of connecting devices to form a network

Personal area network

A **personal area network** (PAN) is a computer network for providing data transmission between devices in an individual's workspace, typically within a range of about 10 metres. Devices might include a desktop computer, laptop, smartphone or tablet. A PAN can be used to transmit data between devices or to connect to a higher-level network or the Internet, with one device taking the role of gateway.

Devices may be connected via a USB, or wirelessly, for example using Bluetooth.

The difference between a wireless PAN and a wireless LAN is essentially that a PAN is usually centred around one individual, while a WLAN serves multiple users.

Case study: Using a PAN

Steven travels to work by train with a laptop and a smartphone. He usually works on his laptop on the journey, but the free connection to the Internet via the train company Wi-Fi is not sufficient for his needs.

When he needs to use the Internet, Steven activates a personal hotspot function on his smartphone. A window on his laptop opens to show all the mobile phone network connections in the vicinity:

Steven selects his smartphone from the list to **tether** his laptop to his phone and types in his password. He is then able to connect to the Internet by logging on to his mobile and using the cellular network.

This is a type of **ad hoc** network, implying a spontaneous, often temporary network of devices communicating with each other directly.

Local area network

A local area network (LAN) connects devices within a building or a group of adjacent buildings on a single site such as a school, university campus, hospital or office building. One LAN can be connected to another over any distance, possibly in another country, through telephone lines and radio waves.

There are two types of local area network:

- Client-server network
- Peer-to-peer network

Client-server architecture

A local area network within an organisation is typically organised as a **client-server network**. It has one or more **servers**, which are computers performing specific functions on the network. Some functions can be combined on a single server, so that for example a single powerful computer can act as both **file server** and **print server**.

The networked devices (called **clients**) are connected to the servers via one or more switches or routers. The connections from the client devices to the switch can be wired or wireless.

A large network may have several servers each performing one or more functions, for example:

- file server, which holds and manages data for all the client computers
- web server, which manages requests to access the internet
- mail server, which manages the email system
- print server, which collects information sent by client computers to a shared printer, and prints everything in an orderly manner

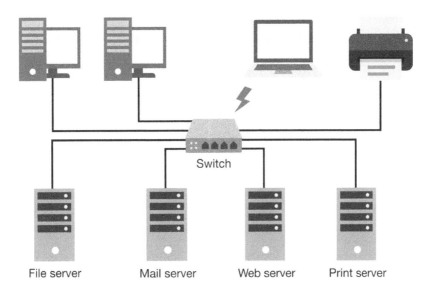

Switch

File server   Mail server   Web server   Print server

Client-server network

 List some advantages of a client-server network.

Peer-to-peer networks

In a peer-to-peer network, there is no central server. Individual computers are connected to each other, either locally or over a wide area network so that they can share files. In a small local area network, such as in a home or small office, a peer-to-peer network is a good choice because:

- it is cheap to set up

- it enables users to share resources such as a printer or router

- it is not difficult to maintain

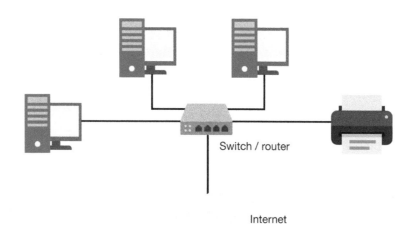

Peer-to-peer network

Peer-to-peer networks are also used by companies providing, for example, video on demand. A problem arises when thousands of people simultaneously want to download the latest episode of a particular TV show. Using a peer-to-peer network, hundreds of computers can be used to hold parts of the video and so share the load.

Wide area network

A wide area network (WAN) spans a large geographical area, which may connect several local area networks. They are commonly established with leased lines from a telecommunications provider. Some WANs are built for one particular organisation; commercial, educational and government organisations all use wide area networks. Other WANs are built by Internet Service Providers (ISPs) to provide connections from an organisation's LAN to the Internet.

Advantages of a WAN

- File servers, email servers, backup servers and database servers can all reside in one Head Office location. All the branch offices can share data through the Head Office server.

- All data are synchronised through the Head Office server, which can provide up-to-date information needed by all branches.

- Backup and support are supplied by Head Office.

- Software resources can be shared, and all offices will get updated versions of software at the same time.

- Workload can be distributed to local offices meaning less staff travel.

Disadvantages of a WAN

- Setup costs are high.

- Security is an issue. If a hacker is able to hack into the system, the personal data of millions of customers may be compromised. Security precautions such as firewalls and secure routers may be expensive to install. Information may be intercepted in transit so needs to be encrypted.

- Troubleshooting problems may be difficult. WANs often use public telephone lines for communications and if a line is broken or fails for some reason, business will be affected.

- Connectivity issues and slow Internet speed may be frustrating for employees and customers.

Virtual private network (VPN)

A corporate VPN

Routers can be used to connect geographically separated offices to form a single network that spans multiple locations. A VPN uses a pair of routers to create a secure virtual private network. Each network uses its router to connect to the Internet, and the routers establish a secure tunnel between themselves to exchange private information.

- This is a much cheaper option than having a leased line to connect offices

- It is more flexible since an employee can use it from anywhere

A corporate VPN is characterised by having the same organisation controlling both endpoints of the VPN. An organisation wanting to set up a VPN signs up with a VPN service provider. The routers at both endpoints connect to this service and are configured to provide a VPN that securely connects the two networks.

All employees needing to use the VPN have a username and password. An employee may initiate a connection from home or from an office geographically separated from the Head Office.

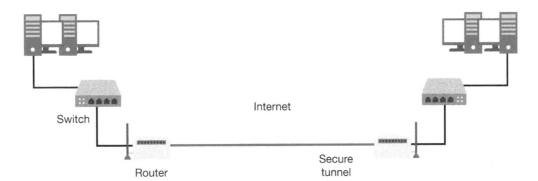

Personal VPN

An individual may also use a VPN service to provide a secure tunnel between their computing device and the VPN service provider. Unlike a corporate VPN, the data is not encrypted all the way to each endpoint. A personal VPN service will be operated by a completely different company from say a bank or a social media site. When the data reaches the VPN service provider's data centre, it is decrypted and sent on to its final destination. (If the data was encrypted by your browser using https, for example, the original encryption is left intact.)

The forwarded data uses an IP address owned by the VPN service so that the user's IP address and location remains anonymous.

A personal VPN offers protection to an individual away from home or the office, using Wi-Fi provided by, for example, a hotel, restaurant, library or train. Even if the Wi-Fi connection has a password, there is no way of knowing who else is accessing the network, intercepting your communications and stealing bank details or other personal information.

When travelling abroad, having a VPN connection means that the user can gain access to websites that are blocked by local service providers. Google and BBC websites, for example, are blocked in China by "The Great Firewall". China has also moved to block VPN.

The Great Wall of China

There are some free VPN providers, but it is important to be careful in choosing a VPN provider. Criminal organisations and malware creators can set up a free VPN service to actively harvest information and either use it or sell it.

Exercises

1. (a) Janine has no Wi-Fi connection in her home. Explain how she can access the Internet on her laptop using her smartphone. [4]

    (b) State what type of network this describes. [1]

2. Joseph is employed by a firm of lawyers. On two days each week, he works from home.

    Explain how he can securely access files on his company server from his home computer. Include in your explanation a list of the devices and connection types that he could use. [6]

3. BetterDeal Insurance is an insurance company specialising in vehicle and home insurance. They have a local area network (LAN) at their Head Office. The network is used to:

    - store personal information about clients and their insurance policies

    - store tables of insurance rates for different types of insurance policy

    - run software to calculate an insurance quote for a specific client

    - perform general administration tasks

    - communicate internally and externally

    (a) Describe how **two** features of a LAN can be used by BetterDeal to carry out required tasks. [4]

    (b) Employees sometimes use laptop computers to connect wirelessly to the LAN while they are in the office.
        Analyse concerns that Daniel, the network manager may have about this practice. [10]

Chapter 12
Factors affecting the choice of network

Objectives

Describe:

- factors affecting the choice of network: user needs, specifications, security, cost, connectivity, implementation, efficiency, compatibility, user experience, productivity

- how the features of a network and its component parts affect the performance of an IT system

Setting up a LAN

Most organisations with more than two or three computers will connect their computers and other devices in a LAN. Why bother networking the computers? It's all about sharing.

User needs

These are some of the advantages to users of networking computers.

Sharing files – once computers are networked, files can either be stored on the server, and any authorised person on the network can download them to their own computer.

Sharing resources – printers, scanners, hard drives and other resources can all be shared. Sharing an Internet connection is one of the main reasons many networks are set up.

Centralised backup – files saved on the server can be backed up on an automatic schedule, for example daily, onto tape or other removeable device. The backup copy will be kept offsite.

Connecting computers in a LAN, with the benefits that it brings, is likely to have a significant effect on productivity. It does not take long to set up and test a small network and it is not likely to have any significant **downtime.** Larger organisations may have hundreds of computers connected in a LAN.

Specifications and cost

Decisions have to be made, based on **user needs**, concerning:

- what type of network to set up
- suitability of different connection types
- security measures
- compatibility with existing systems

Peer-to-peer

For a home network, a peer-to-peer network may be a good choice because it is **inexpensive** to set up and not difficult to maintain. Users will still be able to share resources, but there is no central computer or backup and **security** is much weaker. For these reasons, it is not a good choice for a business.

Client-server

For a business, a client-server network offers the advantages of additional security, with files stored on the server. A second major advantage is that **backups** are done centrally, probably on an automatic schedule, and so the individual users are less likely to lose work in the event of a catastrophe. It will be one person's responsibility to see that backup copies are stored off-site in a secure location (which may be the **cloud**).

A client-server network will be more complex to set up and will need a professional to maintain it. Network users will not be able to change settings or access rights to particular areas; these will all be set by the network manager.

The **cost** of setting up a client-server system is much greater than the cost of setting up a peer-to-peer network.

Security

In many organisations, network security is a major concern. Personal data, by law, has to be kept secure and if it is accidentally destroyed or stolen, fines may be levied by the Information Commissioner's Office (ICO). Moreover, the consequences of data loss can be extremely severe. Statistics in 2018 showed that 93% of companies that lost their data centre for 10 days or more due to a disaster, filed for bankruptcy within one year of the disaster.

Measures to protect data are covered in Learning Aim D.

Connectivity

Devices in the network can be connected by Ethernet or fibre-optic cable, or wirelessly using Wi-Fi.

The implications of each of these connection types was discussed in Chapter 9. The chosen connection types will depend entirely on the nature of the organisation and the nature of the IT systems.

- If speed is a concern, then fibre-optic cable can be used throughout. Its greater cost will be offset by increased **productivity**.
- **Security** is always an issue, and data flowing through a fibre-optic cable cannot easily be intercepted.
- On a factory floor, where machinery may spark or chemicals spill, fibre-optic cable is safer - it is non-flammable and does not overheat.

Working on a factory floor

User experience and implementation

Purchasing, integrating and implementing a new network solution can be stressful. A new network can also be an opportunity to optimise a team's performance and increase productivity. It may decrease individual workloads and result in better client service.

A new network often implies a change to an entire IT system. It's important to understand how compatible it is with existing systems. The level of user experience among employees in changing to a new system may be a factor. A team's background and familiarity with change will have a bearing on implementation and acceptance of a new network system. The whole team's experience with new product integration, and their anxieties about it, should be discussed and resolved.

The timescales for implementing the changeover need to be considered. Training may be required. Ongoing support from the supplier is an important consideration, especially in the period immediately after implementation.

Efficiency and performance

A network manager should have a well-defined testing strategy in order to actively manage the network. The manager needs to know how the network performs under normal operating conditions. He or she should be able to answer questions such as:

- How many users are on the network today, or on an average weekday?

- What is the greatest expense incurred in having the current network?

- What is the peak and average usage of the network backbone?

The insight gained from the answers to these questions should help the network manager to predict network operation under a given load, or anticipate problems created by new services or applications. If network users are reporting frequent problems, the manager needs to be able to evaluate what the problem is and where it is. He or she must determine the level of network services that users will find acceptable.

Network managers may receive complaints from users on a regular basis. These complaints may include poor access times, no access to resources or network downtime. The more information recorded regularly on each user, segment, peripheral, switch, bridge and router, the easier the task of network maintenance becomes.

All of these features of a network affect the **efficiency** and **performance** of an IT system. In addition, the availability of a **fast broadband connection** is probably one of the most crucial factors.

A regular daily, weekly or monthly written record of usage and network problems will show how demand, usage patterns and problems change over time. As an organisation grows or its needs change, the network will need to grow or change accordingly.

Results of regular testing will be invaluable when deciding on upgrades such as the installation of new high-speed broadband or network configurations. Moreover, if documented test results of an existing network are available, continued regular testing of any new network installation will show how effective the new measures are.

Explain how regular testing and recording of network usage, downtime and other problems can help management when it comes to upgrading a network.

Productivity

A network may use a combination of wired and wireless connections. Wireless printers, for example, will require no cables to be run and can be situated anywhere within reach of an electrical outlet and the wireless access point. Wireless all-in-one printers that can print from anywhere in the office will save employees time. An auto power feature which turns the printer on when a job is sent will save on electricity costs.

When connecting to the Internet, productivity will be severely hampered if no broadband connection is available. If a broadband cable already runs down the street outside the office, then it will be inexpensive to install a broadband connection to the Ethernet handoff in the office. If there is no broadband connection in the area, many businesses will not be able to function efficiently.

How features of a network affect the performance of an IT system

The features of different types of network and their component parts affect the performance of the whole IT system. These have been discussed in Chapter 11 and in this chapter. More detail is given below on how specific features of a WAN and VPN can affect performance.

A wide area network

A WAN provides transmission of voice, data, images and videos over a large geographical area.

Companies with branches in different locations, cities or countries can gain huge cost savings and productivity benefits from a WAN. Large organisations such as airlines, railways, banks or telecommunications companies could not operate without a WAN. Many small and medium-sized enterprises (SMEs) also operate WANs. (See Chapter 11 for advantages of a WAN.)

Symmetric and asymmetric broadband connections

A broadband connection to an Internet Service Provider (ISP) is normally **asymmetric**. This means that most of the bandwidth is used for downloading, and only a small portion for uploading. If you test your Internet speed at home, you will find that the upload speed is only a fraction of the download speed. This generally works well since most people spend far more time downloading information from the Internet than uploading.

However, some organisations need a dedicated, symmetrical connection that will give fast data transfer in both directions, regardless of usage. They will benefit from having a leased line, which provides a fast, symmetrical connection.

Using a leased line

A small organisation may use a public telephone line to connect a LAN in one location with a LAN in another location. A leased line is a good choice if the organisation is very large, does financial trading, runs a large website, or needs guaranteed, reliable Internet access 24 hours a day.

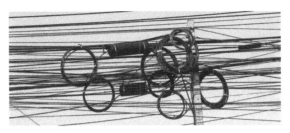

Advantages of a leased line

- It gives very fast upload and download speeds of up to 10 Gbps.

- It is not shared with anybody else, so speeds won't fluctuate.

- With most leased lines, you can change your bandwidth whenever you want, meaning you pay less in quiet periods.

- It is more secure than a shared line.

Disadvantages of a leased line

- It is a very expensive option.

- It can take up to three months to get a leased line installed, whereas regular business broadband can normally be installed in about two weeks.

Case study: Installation of a leased line at Waggon Hotel

Waggon Hotel is an upmarket, well-established hotel in a large town. However, it was experiencing problems with Internet connectivity. Guests frequently complained about poor Wi-Fi availability and speed, and there were ongoing problems with the hotel's online booking systems.

To address these problems, they were recommended to:

- install a 1Gb dedicated fibre leased line to replace the existing low bandwidth ADSL connections

- install 25 wireless access points in the guest rooms, meeting rooms, restaurant and reception area

- install two wireless access points in the outdoor area.

The installation took three months and was costly. However, the hotel management, staff and guests all experienced many benefits.

- They had access to a strong, reliable Wi-Fi signal throughout the entire hotel.

- The hotel received no more complaints regarding the inferior quality of the hotel's Wi-Fi connectivity.

- The hotel experienced a 30% increase in online bookings in the next three months, thanks to the introduction of the dedicated high bandwidth Internet connection.

Discuss two problems that the hotel was facing before the installation of their upgraded Wi-Fi system, and the likely impact of those problems on the profitability of the hotel.

VPN

If security is a major issue, VPN is a cheaper option than a leased line. It's easy to use and a company VPN can be accessed by employees while at home, travelling or in an overseas location to securely transmit and receive data from the company server. All data is end-to-end encrypted.

VPN compatibility issues

VPNs require a connection with high bandwidth for both uploads and downloads, and low latency (see Chapter 13) to function efficiently. Satellite Internet services normally suffer high latencies due to the long distance satellite signals must travel, and satellite bandwidth for uploads is much slower than for downloads.

There are other compatibility issues which may prevent connection to a VPN. In some cases, a firewall may block the VPN when a user tries to connect to the VPN server. If the user is trying to connect to the VPN from home, their router may need a router firmware update to be compatible with the VPN.

> **"Unable to establish the VPN Connection" (error 800)**

Exercises

1. BetterBuild is a large construction company building more than 1,000 new homes every year. The company has a broadband connection at their Head Office which is used for office email and web browsing.

   BetterBuild use cloud storage to save all their data, rather than holding it on the main server. All branches in the company have access to this cloud storage facility. Uploading data is very slow.

   (a) Explain why, with their existing broadband connection, BetterBuild experiences problems with uploading documents but not with downloading. [3]

   (b) BetterBuild have decided to replace their existing connection with a leased line.
   Describe **three** impacts that this is likely to have on the company. [6]

2. JCH is a small firm of accountants with only three employees. At the moment they have a peer-to-peer network. The managing director has decided they should upgrade to a client-server network.

   (a) Describe **two** benefits that this will bring to the company. [4]

   (b) Identify **three** different connection methods that could be used to connect the office computers.
   Describe **one** advantage of each. [9]

3. Tom is the network manager at Henley School. He has been receiving complaints about the performance of the network from staff, on behalf of themselves and their pupils. Funds have been made available to upgrade the network.

   (a) Describe **two** measures Tom should take in order to assess the problems with the current network. [4]

   (b) Analyse the factors that Tom should consider when choosing an upgraded network configuration. [10]

Chapter 13
Features and processes of data transmission

Objectives

Describe:

- protocols used to govern and control data transmission for: email, voice and video calls over the Internet, web pages, secure payment systems
- security issues and considerations when transmitting data over different connection types and networks
- factors affecting bandwidth and latency
- the implications of bandwidth and latency on the use and performance of an IT system
- types of compression: lossy, lossless
- the applications and implications of data compression
- the use and implications of codecs when using and transmitting audio and video in digital format

Protocols

A protocol is a set of rules defining common methods of data communication. These rules need to be standard across all devices in order for them to communicate with each other. A protocol will specify, for example:

- the format of data packets
- the addressing system
- transmission speed
- error-checking procedures being used

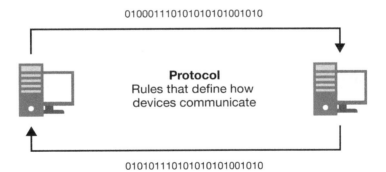

Email protocols

A **mail server** acts as a virtual post office for all incoming and outgoing emails. The server routes mail according to its database of local network users' email addresses as it comes and goes, and stores it until it can be retrieved.

- **Post Office Protocol (v3) (POP3)** is responsible for retrieving emails from a mail server that temporarily stores your incoming mail. When emails are retrieved, they are transferred to your local computer, tablet or mobile phone, and deleted from the server. As a result, if you are using different devices to access email via POP3, you will find that they don't synchronise the same emails on each device.

- **Internet Message Access Protocol (IMAP)** is an email protocol that is designed to keep emails on the server, thus maintaining synchronicity between devices.

- **Simple Mail Transfer Protocol (SMTP)** is used to transfer outgoing emails from one server to another or from an email client to the server when sending an email.

Email protocols

Voice and video calls over the Internet

Voice over Internet Protocol (VoIP) allows users to make free, or very low cost, telephone calls over the Internet. In a business using VoIP, an employee can call any telephone in the world and anyone can call the VoIP telephone - regardless of what equipment or network the person uses.

Because VoIP uses digital Internet technologies, many features and services that are very expensive using traditional telephone technology are available free. These include:

- voicemails sent to your email

- call diverts

- call conferencing

Software such as Skype may be used to make voice and video calls to anywhere in the world. Once the software has been downloaded, all that is needed is a broadband connection to the Internet, speakers, microphone and webcam.

Web page protocols

HTTP (HyperText Transfer Protocol) is the standard protocol for browsers to render web pages. It defines how messages are formatted and transmitted, and what actions Web servers and browsers should take in response to various commands. When you enter a URL (web page address) in your browser, this sends an HTTP command to the Web server directing it to fetch and transmit the requested Web page.

TCP/IP (Transmission Control Protocol/Internet Protocol) is a suite of transmission protocols used worldwide to connect Internet devices on the Internet.

TCP defines how applications can create channels of communication across a network. It specifies how a message is assembled into smaller packets before being transmitted over the internet and reassembled in the right order at the destination address.

IP defines how to address and route each packet to make sure it reaches the right destination. Each gateway computer on the network checks this IP address to determine where to forward the message.

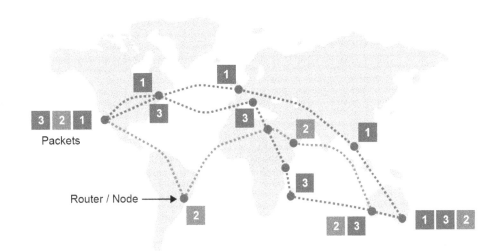

Routing data packets across the Internet

HTTPS (secure protocol) encrypts the information so that it cannot be understood if it is hacked. Banks and many other organisations always use the https protocol.

Data sent over a standard Internet connection is inherently insecure. Organisations needing to keep personal data secure may use a VPN, which provides a secure tunnel, with all data encrypted, between routers.

NFC (Near Field Communication) is a communication protocol set which can be used to transfer data between devices within a few centimetres of each other. This can be used for transferring photographs, mobile ticketing and in many places to make payments by tapping a smartphone on a credit card terminal (NFC receiver) to send payment automatically.

In 2018 there were three main NFC payment services: Apple Pay for iPhone or Mac computer users, Android Pay for Android phones and Samsung Pay for Samsung users. Each of these systems requires an additional level of security before payment can be made – this could be a PIN or a biometric lock. Using the latter requires a fingerprint or face scan to authorise payment. It is at least as secure as any other card payment system.

Secure payment systems

There are more than 300 payment schemes in the world.

Credit card and debit card payments, bank transfers and PayPal are examples of secure, online payment systems. All payments are made to websites using the **https** protocol. This is particularly important when payments are being made or money transferred, since if the data is hacked by a cyber-criminal, the user could be defrauded of large amounts of money.

Secure payment systems often have effective anti-fraud tools to help customers recognise irregular transactions and reduce the risk of payment fraud.

Factors affecting available bandwidth

Bandwidth, measured in megabits per second (Mbps), is the main factor affecting network performance. The more bandwidth available, the faster data is transferred. On a shared Internet connection, the total bandwidth (e.g. 10 Mbps) is shared among all users and devices.

For example, a standard video call on Skype could take between 0.3 and 1.5 Mbps of bandwidth. A single VoIP call takes up to 1Mbps. As a business grows and more and more people start using the Internet for different purposes, response time and data transmission becomes appreciably slower.

Factors affecting latency

Latency is the time delay between the moment that transmission of the first byte or packet of a communication starts, and when it is received at its destination. It is a function of the time it takes the information to travel from source to destination. There are different factors influencing latency:

- **Transmission medium:** Fibre-optic cable will transmit data much faster than coaxial cables

- **Bandwidth:** The more bandwidth available, the faster data is transferred

- **Connection:** Additional network latency is caused when traffic is routed through Internet servers and other backbone devices

- **Internet traffic load** at busy times of day

- **Distance:** In wireless transmission when satellite links are used, distances of more than 100,000 km are involved, and you can sometimes see the result on live TV when a presenter in a studio talks to a reporter at a distant location

Transmitting via satellite

Implications of bandwidth and latency on performance

In an organisation using cloud computing, where software is held in the cloud rather than on a local router, broadband is essential. Moreover, if too many people are using a single broadband connection, upload and download speeds will be badly affected and performance will suffer. This will be frustrating for employees and customers alike.

Latency is a similar issue – the type of connection will affect performance. Satellite connections used for VoIP calls may make it difficult to communicate effectively, with a delay between someone speaking and the other person hearing. A leased line with a dedicated broadband connection and fibre-optic cables will provide lightning fast speed. For organisations handling financial transactions, this may be essential.

Data compression

File compression techniques were developed to reduce the storage space of files on disk. With disk storage becoming larger and cheaper, this is less important these days, but the reduction of file size has become even more important in the sharing and transmission of data. Internet Service Providers (ISPs) and mobile phone networks impose limits and charges on bandwidth. Images on websites need to be in a compressed format to enable a web page to load quickly – on a slow connection, music and video streaming must take advantage of compression in order to reduce buffering. (In streaming audio or video from the Internet, buffering refers to downloading a certain amount of data before starting to play the music or movie. It is needed when the playback speed is greater than the download speed.)

Files sent by email often need to be compressed in order to fit within an attachment limit.

Compression can be either **lossy**, where unnecessary information is removed from the original file, or **lossless**. Lossless compression retains all information required to replicate the original file exactly.

Lossy compression

Lossy compression works by removing non-essential information. The two **JPG** images below are clearly identifiable as the same, but one has been heavily compressed, displaying digital artefacts as a consequence. The subject of the image can be made out well but its quality suffers when it is too heavily compressed.

Original image 310KB   *Heavily compressed image 5.7KB*

Compression of sound and video

The compression of sound and video works in a similar way. **MP3** files use lossy compression to remove frequencies too high for most of us to hear and to remove quieter sounds that are played at the same time as louder sounds. The resulting file is about 10% of original size, meaning that 1 minute of MP3 audio equates to roughly 1MB in size.

Voice is transmitted over the telephone network using lossy compression and although we have no problem in understanding what the other person is saying, we can recognise the difference in quality of a voice over a phone rather than in person. The apparent difference is lost data.

Lossless compression

Lossless compression works by recording patterns in data rather than the actual data. Using these patterns and a set of instructions on how to use them, the computer can reverse the procedure and reassemble an image, sound or text file with exact accuracy and no data is lost. This is most important with the compression of text or program files for example, where a single lost character would result in an error in the programming code. A pixel with a slightly different colour, on the other hand, is not of great consequence in most cases. Lossless compression usually results in a much larger file than a lossy file, but one that is still significantly smaller than the original.

What type of compression is likely to be used for the following: a website image, a zipped file of long text documents and images, a PDF instruction manual?

Codecs

A **codec** (short for **co**der/**dec**oder) is software used for converting analogue signals into digital form, or for converting between digital signal formats.

An audio codec converts analogue audio signals into digital signals for transmission or storage. A receiving device converts the digital signals back to analogue form using an audio decoder for playback. An example of this are the codecs used in the sound cards of personal computers. A video codec accomplishes the same task for video signals.

A codec may also compress the data to reduce transmission bandwidth or storage space. Compression may be lossy or lossless.

Many popular codecs are lossy. Although quality is reduced, depending on the settings used, files using this type of compression can be virtually indistinguishable from the original uncompressed sound or image.

Exercises

1. (a) Explain what is meant by a **transmission protocol**. [4]
    (b) Draw a diagram showing what protocols are used when sending emails over a WAN. [4]
    (c) Describe how the **https** protocol ensures that data transmission is secured during data transmission. [2]
    (d) (i) Identify **one** other electronic method which ensures that an employee working from home can send digital data securely to her Head Office. [1]
    (ii) Describe the method that you identified in part d (i). [2]

2. Theresa needs to send a folder containing two large text files and several images, to a colleague via email.

    (a) Explain why the data may need to be compressed before being sent. [2]
    (b) Explain the difference between lossy and lossless compression. [2]
    (c) Explain, giving reasons, which type of compression will be appropriate for Theresa's files. [3]

3. **https** is a transmission protocol used to send secure transmissions.

    (a) Name another protocol which is used to make secure payments using a smartphone and a portable credit card terminal. [1]
    (b) Describe how the user makes a payment using this system. [2]
    (c) Describe a security measure used to ensure that the payment method is secure and cannot be misused by someone who has stolen the smartphone. [2]

4. (a) Describe what is meant by **latency**. [2]
    (b) Explain why this effect will be far greater when satellite transmission is used than when a fibre-optic connection is used. [2]

Chapter 14
Drawing system diagrams

Objectives

- Draw a diagram to show how an IT system works

(*This topic is not mentioned on the specification but the chapter gives practice in answering this type of question, which is often asked in the external exam.*)

Purpose of a system diagram

Computer systems generally consist of several devices connected to each other and to the outside world by some means or other. For example, a single PC at home may be connected to a printer, microphone, and external speakers. It will probably be connected to a router with a built in Wireless Access Point (WAP) to enable the user to connect to the Internet. A WAP has a range of about 20 metres indoors and more outdoors.

A system diagram shows:

- Devices and systems that could be used
- Devices to be connected and the connection types used
- The flow of data through the system
- Annotations indicating the information and data to be passed between systems, devices and users

Connections

- Connection types include:
- Ethernet, generally used to connect networked devices in a Local Area Network
- Fibre-optic cable
- Wi-Fi
- Bluetooth
- Mobile (cell) network
- USB connector

Example 1

Megan receives an email with an attachment on her home PC from a colleague's mobile phone. She prints out the attachment on the printer attached to the PC. Draw a diagram to show the devices used, connection types and flow of data.

Solution

Here is one way of showing this system:

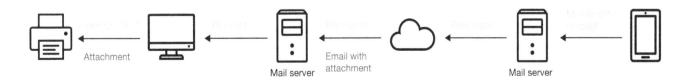

Redraw the diagram using boxes instead of icons. Assume the email is sent from a PC rather than a mobile phone.

Example 2

Mishal is at a music festival. She uses her smartphone, tapping it on the food seller's NFC (near-field communication) credit card terminal to establish a wireless connection, (creating an ad hoc network) to pay for food using her credit card. The NFC-powered terminal sends an authorisation request to Mishal's bank, which authorises the payment. A record of the transaction is sent using the mobile/cell network to the LAN at the main office. It is downloaded by the sales clerk, Nadine, to her PC.

Using NFC and mobile payment

Draw an annotated diagram showing the devices to be connected and the connection types.

Solution

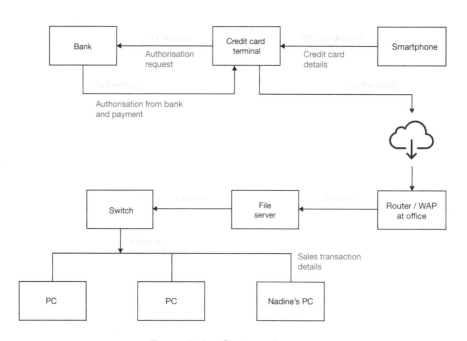

Example 2 – System diagram

Complete the labelling of the data flows through the system.

Example 3

A retail chain selling car parts holds stock in a central warehouse. Each store in the chain has its own **local area network** with a **PC** at each checkout, connected to the **company server** using an **Internet-based Virtual Private Network** (**VPN**). To access the VPN, a client computer connects to the nearest service provider's **access point**.

When a customer comes to the store to buy a part which is not on the store shelves, the sales assistant uses a PC to connect to the company database, held on the server, to ascertain whether the part is available.

Draw a diagram to represent this system.

Solution

Start by drawing the **hardware components** mentioned in the scenario (shown in black).

Then label the **type of connection** (shown in blue). Finally, label the **data flow** (shown in red).

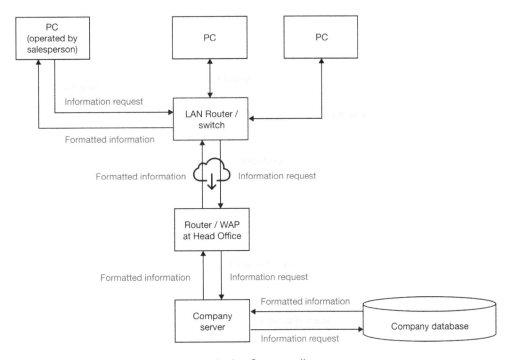

Example 3 – System diagram

Note that there are no hard and fast rules about what symbols to use for hardware items, or even how much detail you should include. Be guided by the number of marks allocated to the question.

Example 4

A customer orders some books from an online bookstore using a mobile phone. The order is processed by the company's ordering system.

The customer receives an acknowledgement via email.

The order details are sent to the main warehouse via Internet-based VPN. When the order is dispatched, an email is sent to the customer advising delivery date.

Draw a diagram showing how information flows through the system. Show the devices and connection types at each stage.

Solution

This time, detail of how the ordering system connects to the VPN is not shown. Icons are used for the mobile phone and shopping cart, but this is not necessary – boxes could be used.

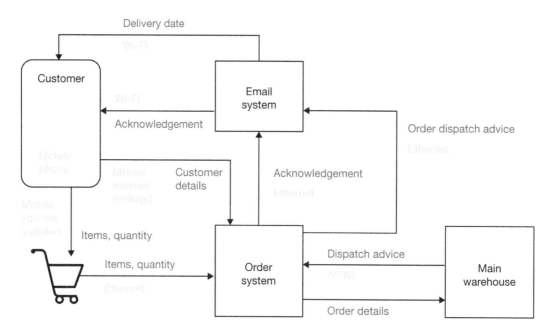

Example 4 – System diagram

Exercises

1. Royle's is a small catering company which employs many people working from home. Every Monday morning, the owner, manager and all employees join in an online meeting using Skype for Business.

    Amy is an employee working from home. She has a PC, webcam, microphone and speakers, so that she can see and hear the others who have joined the meeting.

    Draw and annotate a diagram to show the devices and connection types between Amy and the manager's PC, which is part of the office Local Area Network.

    Your diagram should show devices and connection types used to connect them. [6]

2. A fast food outlet serves a range of food and drinks such as hamburgers, hot dogs and soft drinks. The system works as follows:

    1. A customer places an order using a touch screen at an online order point.

    2. The payment amount is displayed and the customer pays using cash or credit/debit card.

    3. The order is sent to a PC in the kitchen.

    4. The order is recorded to update the quantities in stock.

    5. Every day, items are ordered from a supplier.

    (a) Draw and annotate a diagram to represent this system, showing devices and systems that could be used, connection types used to connect devices and the flow of data through the system. [8]

    (b) State **two** items of data that must be held on the stock control file for each item so that Step 5 can be carried out. [2]

Operating online

In this section:

Chapter 15
Online systems

Objectives

Describe:

- the personal and professional uses and applications of cloud storage and cloud computing
- the impact and implications on individuals and organisations of using **cloud storage** and computing

Personal uses of cloud storage

Cloud storage comes in many different forms. Dropbox is an example of a cloud storage and sync service available for MACs, PCs and most mobile devices. It has a free version which gives the user up to 2GB of cloud storage.

Once you sign up for an account, a Dropbox folder appears in your list of folders, for example in Windows File Explorer, just like any other folder. By default, Dropbox will synchronise (**sync**) a copy of all your files to the Dropbox folder on your computer. *Selective Sync* lets you choose which folders you want to keep on your hard drive, and which folders you only want to keep online in the cloud.

For example, if you do not want large media files synced (automatically copied) to your laptop, taking up all the disk space, you can disable syncing to your laptop, but still access all these files from your PC or through an online portal.

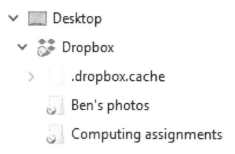

You can:

- create as many folders as you like within the Dropbox folder
- save files and folders from your PC to a Dropbox folder
- share any of these folders with friends or colleagues who have accounts with Dropbox
- upload photos and videos to Dropbox directly from your phone, and then delete them from your phone to free up space

Shared storage space in the cloud makes it easy to share large files with friends or colleagues. It also ensures that you will never lose files or precious photos and documents you have stored, since backup is done automatically by the cloud service provider. Dropbox and other cloud storage providers also offer enterprise level facilities for businesses.

Personal uses of cloud services

You may already be using cloud services. If, for example, you use Gmail or Googlemail, you are already using a cloud application. Google is hosting it, and you are accessing it through your browser as a client.

You may also be using some of these cloud computing applications or services:

Google G Suite: A productivity and collaboration tool, which includes GoogleDocs, a free word processor that you do not have to load on your computer, but access via the Internet in the same way you access your email account. It allows you to share documents for viewing and editing, and allows multiple users to collaborate simultaneously on a project over the web.

Microsoft Office 365 / OneDrive: A stripped down collaborative version of MS Office, free to use through a browser. OneDrive provides users free cloud storage of up to 5GB in 2019.

Flickr: A popular photo-sharing and hosting service that allows people to share each other's photos. You can create albums tag and organise photos, add notes and search for photos.

Apple iCloud: iCloud is built into every Apple device. Photos, files, notes and more are automatically saved, updated and available. All users get 5GB of free iCloud storage and can add more at any time.

The Internet of Things

The **Internet of Things (IoT)** is the term used to describe the network of physical devices, vehicles, home appliances, and other items with embedded software, sensors and actuators. Wireless connection to the Internet enables these things to connect, collect and exchange data.

Home automation, **wearable technology** and **appliances with remote monitoring capabilities** are all applications used by individuals.

Internet of things connected via the cloud

Uses of cloud computing

There are three distinct kinds of services provided via the cloud (i.e. the Internet):

- **Applications**, referred to as Software as a Service (SaaS)
- **Platforms**, referred to as Platform as a Service (PaaS)
- **Infrastructure**, referred to as Infrastructure as a Service (IaaS)

Software as a Service (SaaS)

Traditionally, software such as word-processing, spreadsheet and presentation software was purchased on a CD. The user inserted the CD, typed in a unique serial number printed on the label, and loaded the software onto their computer. In an organisation, this process was repeated for every computer.

The next step forward came when a multi-user software licence was purchased online, and the software could simply be downloaded onto each machine.

Using the cloud, once the software licence is purchased, the software is not downloaded to any of the computers. It remains with the software provider in the cloud. The user, either personally or professionally, has access to their version of the software with personalised settings, and all the data that they create. They can log on to the software from any computer, anywhere in the world.

Using a cloud-based application means that the computing manager of an organisation does not have to worry about installing the application on new machines or applying upgrades. For a small monthly fee, the application provider takes care of all the detail. They will ensure that the system runs on the company's operating system platform.

Accounting services are commonly provided by cloud applications. Sage is one of many companies providing such a service for a monthly fee.

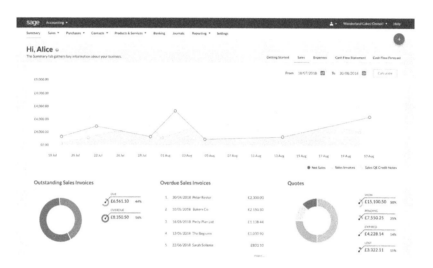

An online accounting package

Platform as a Service (PaaS)

This service provides an organisation with a complete, remote, functional virtual machine fully configured to run an application. This is most commonly used to host a company's website. An organisation using this type of service takes the responsibility of customising applications to run on the website or platform, and the PaaS provider maintains the platform, including the operating system and the hardware on which the website or other service runs.

An organisation using PaaS can develop their own customised software to run on the remote platform. They can also make use of specialised software such as data storage, online order processing and credit card payment systems included by the PaaS provider.

Infrastructure as a Service (IaaS)

IaaS typically provides access to networking services, computers (virtual or on dedicated hardware) and data storage space. It is up to the user to manage and configure the remote computer in whatever way they need. The user decides what software to put onto the virtual machine and how the virtual disks are organised. The IaaS provider will provide storage and other resources as they are needed.

Impact and implications on individuals

Remote working is one of the most revolutionary trends of the past decade, largely enabled by cloud computing and storage. Many employees tied to a particular office location are forced to live far away from their place of work, because of the high cost of housing in urban areas. An employee may have to leave the house before 7am and not get home until 7pm or later. Being able to work from home on at least two days a week is a hugely attractive option, and numerous surveys have found that workers would choose flexible working over a pay rise. Apart from the flexibility of working at home, the amount saved on not having to commute every day can offset the lack of a pay rise.

Staff working at home via the cloud can access the same shared files and use the same software as they would in the office. They can fit home commitments such as taking children to school and picking them up, around their work schedule. Not having to spend wasted hours commuting gives them more time to spend with their families. They do not arrive home exhausted after a 12-hour day and are able to achieve a better work-life balance.

According to surveys, almost all employees believe that mobile technology has a positive impact on their overall performance. As well as being able to work from home, they can use laptops and other mobile devices form almost any location worldwide to keep in contact with the office.

On the negative side, the distractions of being at home, faced with chores that need doing can affect concentration. Being able to check incoming texts and emails on a smartphone or check the latest personal Facebook or Twitter posts may also affect productivity.

Working from home has many advantages

Impact and implications on organisations

Advantages of cloud computing

There are many ways in which organisations can benefit from using cloud storage and cloud computing. Here are some of them.

Cost: Cloud storage is typically less costly than buying sufficient disk storage or equivalent to store all the applications, organisational data and customer data.

Data security: Data held on a server on the premises is always at risk. Cloud providers have data centres located in several different geographical areas, with multiple redundancies so that data is always safe even if one data centre is catastrophically destroyed.

Reliability: Cloud services and storage are more reliable than in-house applications. System maintenance, software updates and backups are all taken care of.

Scalability: As an organisation expands, its storage needs will grow accordingly. When a 1TB server is close to filling up, should the company buy another 1Tb server at huge expense, which may not be used to capacity for many years? If the data needs become less, you cannot return the server and get a refund. With cloud storage, the organisation pays for the storage they are actually using, and this expands and contracts according to demand.

Flexibility: Organisations which experience very high activity on certain days of the year may find that a website held on a company server cannot cope with the extra demands, and the users may then experience very slow response times. A cloud-based website will allocate the necessary resources to cope with any level of activity.

Global access: Applications and data held in the cloud are available from anywhere in the world where there is an Internet connection. Employees working for an organisation with offices in different towns can all access the same software and data, and can access them from home or while travelling.

Drawbacks of cloud computing

Internet connection speed and reliability

Without a fast broadband connection, users in the office may find that it takes much longer to download data and perform application tasks than when everything is held on the local server.

If the Internet connection fails, no one in the office can access the cloud applications or data if synchronised versions are not held locally. Business could grind to a halt until the connection is restored. Contingency plans are needed to cope with this situation.

Security threats

Data transmitted over the Internet is vulnerable to hackers. The best protection is to educate all employees:

- to use strong passwords on all their devices
- to recognise possible phishing attacks
- not to open email attachments from unknown sources

Exercises

1. Fraser's is an online retail company selling children's toys, games and puzzles. Trade is fairly steady throughout the year but peaks massively during the two weeks before Christmas. Their website, hosted on a local server, incorporates an online ordering system.

   (a) Explain two problems that the uneven demand through the year may cause. [4]

   (b) Describe **three** advantages to Fraser's of moving to a cloud-based system using Platform as a Service (PaaS) and Software as a Service (SaaS). [6]

2. MGTech is a web design company which designs and hosts websites for its customers. Much of their management and design software, and all of their shared data, are held in the cloud.

   (a) Describe **two** advantages of holding shared data in the cloud. [4]

   (b) Describe a possible drawback of using SaaS. [2]

3. (a) Explain **two** differences between **cloud storage** and **cloud computing**. [4]

   (b) Describe **one** way in which an individual may make use of:

      (i) Cloud storage [2]

      (ii) Cloud computing [2]

Chapter 16
Use and selection of online systems

Objectives

Describe:

- systems that enable and support remote working: VPNs, remote desktop technologies
- factors affecting the use and selection of online systems: security, cost, ease of use, features, connectivity

Changing work styles

Remote working means working somewhere other than in the office – often from home, or while travelling. The evolution of technology has meant that all employees no longer need to work in the office on desktop computers provided by the IT department.

Instead, many employees work on a mixture of personal and company-owned devices, often from home, for at least part of each week. They can also use mobile devices while commuting to work, visiting other branches of the company, or attending conferences anywhere in the world. Using cloud technologies, **virtual private networks** (**VPNs**) and remote desktop technologies, employees can connect to and interact with a computer in another location via an internal network or the Internet. They can hold online meetings using video conferencing.

Use of a VPN

VPNs were considered in Section B, Chapter 11. A VPN securely connects geographically separated computers in organisational offices by encrypting all communications between them.

This is a major step in preventing the theft of data which could otherwise occur if it is transmitted over a public network such as the Internet.

Remote desktop technologies

Remote desktop software allows a user to connect to and interact with a computer in another location via a WAN, VPN or the Internet. The user can see and control a connected PC or laptop as though they were sitting directly in front of it. It can be used, for example, for demonstrations, collaborative working or trouble-shooting by technical support.

This technology enables an organisation to outsource the technical IT support occasionally needed both by employees working in the office and those working at home or at a remote location.

Using this type of software, it is possible to:

- display the remote computer screen on your own screen in real time
- use your own keyboard and mouse to control the remote screen
- allow a remote user, for example a technical support worker, complete access to and control over your computer
- connect either via an internal network or IP address

Case study: RemoteConnekt

Reviews of remote desktop software can be found online. Here is a typical summary of such software:

RemoteConnekt   4.5 ☆☆☆☆☆ (739)

RemoteConnekt software provides easy-to-use, scalable, and secure software to connect to and monitor any device, anywhere in the world. From desktop-to-desktop, desktop-to-mobile, mobile-to-mobile, or to unattended devices like servers and IoT devices, RemoteConnekt allows you to service and support the widest array of platforms and technologies.

One review of the software included these points:

"What I like about this application is the simple way that it allows me to connect with others with a single click… it is super intuitive… it is a vital tool when working with complex systems and there are no experts or advisers available who can provide face-to-face assistance…"

"Sometimes the connection goes down or it becomes very slow during communication … it requires a very good Internet connection."

"I currently use an administrative system and our advisors and experts do not work in our office, so I connect with them through RemoteConnekt . They have managed to solve various urgent problems in record time."

A second reviewer wrote:

"I use RemoteConnekt personally to connect to my computers remotely. This allows me to have access to the computer and the network at home while I am at work."

"In our company we all use RemoteConnekt to connect from home to the work computer and vice versa. I also use it from time to time to access the network while I'm away and to transfer files between computers. I've used it several times to connect remotely from home, access my work computer and solve programming problems for co-workers."

"It has an easy-to-use interface and a very good connection to the server."

Q1
  (a) Summarise the ways in which the two different reviewers use remote access technology software.

  (b) One reviewer mentions a problem which the second reviewer does not have. Suggest a reason for this, and a solution to the problem.

Factors affecting the use and selection of online systems

Security

Security is a major issue to be considered. In a post in 2018, Facebook CEO Mark Zuckerberg said that *"Security isn't a problem you ever fully solve."* Under the new **General Data Protection Regulation (GDPR)** which came into force in May 2018, strengthening the existing Data Protection Act, it is a legal requirement to keep personal data private and secure. There are other very good reasons why a company cannot afford to have its data hacked, misused or stolen. Security breaches are extremely damaging in terms of financial and reputational costs.

The increasing use of mobile devices such as laptops, tablets and smartphones for work purposes increases the risk of security breaches. Employees may lose devices or use insecure Wi-Fi hotspots to unwittingly download infected content or apps.

Use of multiple devices poses a security risk

The use of a VPN will reduce security risks when employees work at home or while travelling.

Cost

The relatively small cost of leasing a VPN has to be compared with the potential risks of a security breach when employees are working remotely, the costs of which could be enormous.

The cost of using remote desktop technology to outsource technical or software support, for example, will almost certainly be outweighed by the time saved, lower levels of frustration and additional productivity by employees who are able to get immediate help with problems when required.

Ease of use and features

The choice between different systems supporting remote working may be influenced by the user interface and how easy it is to use. The different features offered by the software, such as demonstrations, web conferencing, collaborative working or trouble-shooting will also influence the choice. It is not worth paying for a lot of features which will never be used, but it must have the features that the organisation needs.

Connectivity

A fast broadband connection will be required to enable satisfactory speed and response time.

Impact and implications of remote working

There are many potential benefits to an organisation brought about by the enabling of remote working. Some of these benefits are listed below.

Productivity

A study involving 8,000 global employees and employers conducted by Vodafone in 2016 found that three-quarters of companies worldwide have already adopted flexible working policies and 61% of them believe that it had increased their company's profits. More than 80% reported that productivity was boosted by flexible hours rather than reduced by them.

Increased pool of potential employees

Cloud computing enables organisations to select employees from a wider pool, geographically far from the office, who can work mainly from home. It is often difficult to find employees to fill posts that require a high level of experience or technical knowledge. Advertising a position with flexible working conditions to a wider audience can potentially attract just the right person. In addition, cloud computing means that instead of spending thousands of pounds on expensive newspaper advertisements, jobs can be advertised for nothing on the company's own website, or inexpensively on specialised websites.

Increased employee loyalty

Employees who are able to customise their work schedule to balance their professional and personal lives are likely to feel grateful for these benefits. This will generate increased loyalty to the company, motivating them to work harder and making them less likely to leave. A high turnover of staff is costly and has a detrimental effect on productivity.

Fewer sick days

Employees working from home are generally able to incorporate more exercise into their day and have better health as a result. They are less likely to take personal days off because of minor health problems, or to go to doctor's or dentist's appointments during 'working hours'.

Decreased overhead costs

Office space, especially in prime urban locations, is expensive. Employees who work remotely do not need office space, supplies and other facilities. It may be sufficient to supply a few spare desks so that employees spending only part of their time in the office can "hot-desk".

Exercises

1. Harden's, a firm of accountants, is about to install new software to enable it to carry out accounting functions for its clients. The software supplier offers Harden's the option of paying for remote desktop technology to help employees with any problems they experience with the software.

   (a) Describe what is meant by **remote desktop technology**. [3]

   (b) Describe features of the software that will potentially be useful in solving employees' problems with the software. [3]

   (c) Describe **two** factors that Harden's should consider before signing up to this option. [4]

2. Evaluate the benefits to an organisation of allowing employees to work from home instead of coming in to the office every day. [10]

Chapter 17
Interacting with online communities

Objectives

Describe:

- the features of online communities and the implications of their widespread use for organisations and individuals

- ways of communicating and interacting with online communities: social media, blog, microblog, vlog, wiki, chatrooms, instant messaging, podcasts, forums

- the implications for individuals of using and accessing online communities:
  - user experience – ease of use, performance, availability, accessibility
  - meeting needs, cost, privacy, security

Using social media

Social media is a set of online communication software tools to enable people to interact with one another, get and share information.

 Name some social media sites that you use. How much time do you spend on social media?

Ways of communicating and interacting with online communities
Blogs, microblogs and vlogs

A blog (short for "web log") is an online journal or informational piece of writing posted on a website, with the most recent post appearing first. Many companies integrate a blog into their websites to share information and encourage feedback from viewers. A blog could, for example, share food recipes, provide the latest news on a company product, or give daily updates on an individual's travels around the world.

A microblog is a type of blog that lets users publish short text updates. Platforms that enable users to do this include Instagram, Facebook and Twitter as well as instant messaging services.

A vlog (short for video log) is a blog that takes the form of a video. Some successful "YouTubers" make a fortune from posting videos that are watched by millions of viewers. YouTube's algorithm picks up on successful videos and directs viewers to the uploader's other vlogs. The downside for the vlogger is that success depends on day-by-day reliability, and unless daily videos are posted, rankings tumble.

Case study: The ups and downs of being a vlogger

Matt Lees, a popular YouTube vlogger, started 2013 with 1000 subscribers, which rapidly increased to 90,000. The pressure to keep up the daily vlog became intense, and his health began to suffer.

"Human brains really aren't designed to be interacting with hundreds of people every day" said Lees. *"When you've got thousands of people giving you direct feedback on your work, you really get the sense that*

something in your mind just snaps. We just aren't built to handle empathy and sympathy on that scale. What started out as being the most fun job imaginable quickly slid into something that felt deeply bleak and lonely."

Q2 **Summarise the downsides to (a) vloggers and (b) subscribers of the pressures and compulsion to create or read daily blogs.**

Wikis

A **wiki** is a collaborative website that comprises the work of many authors. The most famous wiki is Wikipedia, a free online encyclopaedia. It is hosted by the Wikimedia Foundation, a non-profit organisation, and contains millions of articles written in many different languages. Most of the articles are not reviewed by a moderator. However, readers can edit, improve and re-publish articles. It is an invaluable free reference source for millions of users around the globe, funded by voluntary contributions from users.

WikiLeaks is another famous wiki that publishes secret information and news leaks provided by anonymous sources. These are often political in nature, and much of it is considered illegal under the Official Secrets Act or equivalent in other countries. High-profile whistle-blowers such as Julian Assange and Chelsea Manning used WikiLeaks to publicise what they considered to be illegal or unethical behaviour by the US government.

Chatrooms

A **chatroom** is technically a channel, the term "room" being used as a metaphor to promote the idea of chatting to someone else. A chatroom provides a venue for communities of users with a common interest to communicate in real time by typing text onscreen.

Instant messaging

Instant messaging is similar to a chatroom in that it allows the user to chat with someone in real time using screen-based text. The difference is that conversation is private, accessible only for a group of invited individuals. Typically, the instant messaging service alerts you whenever somebody on your contact list is online. You can then initiate a chat session with that person.

Instant messaging is often used by software companies to offer help and advice to users having problems with the software, instead of using a helpline phone service. It is also used by companies when a user logs on to their site, to encourage them to buy the particular product that they are reading about.

Q3 **Describe two advantages of using instant messaging rather than a telephone helpline when you need help or want to report a problem with a product.**

Podcasts

Podcasting is a way of distributing digital media files (usually audio but sometimes video) via the Internet. Once a podcast has been downloaded, it can be listened to on a computer or portable device. By 2018, more than half a million podcasts, mostly free, were available in more than 100 languages.

A **podcast** is a series of files which can be listened to or viewed using a podcasting application called a podcatcher. Popular podcatchers designed for use with smartphones include iCatcher, Downcast, Google Podcasts and Apple's Podcasts app. People often listen to podcasts through headphones while walking, running, or travelling by car or train.

Unlike traditional radio, podcasters can produce shows in their living room on any topic they choose. Podcast listeners can subscribe to a particular show or series.

Forums

An Internet **forum** or message board is an online discussion site where people post and respond to messages. A forum can have several subforums, and each subforum may have several topics. Within a topic, each new conversation is known as a **thread**.

A forum is similar to a chatroom, but messages are often longer and are at least temporarily archived so that you can look back through a thread.

Posted messages on some forums are checked by a moderator before being posted.

Reasons why individuals use online communities

The reasons why people use social media vary according to the particular platform, and the number of hours spent on it.

According to a survey, the top four reasons that people use social media are to:

- stay in touch with what their friends are doing (42%).
- stay up-to-date with news and current events (41%).
- fill up spare time (39%).
- find funny or entertaining content (37%).

 What other reasons are there for using social media?

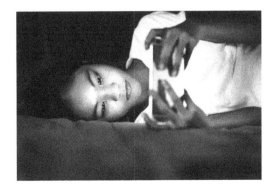

A smartphone screen can disrupt sleep patterns in children and adults

User experience

Having such a mass of information and opportunities to comment and connect with others can be a mixed blessing. It spreads knowledge and understanding, but it also provides endless opportunities to waste time and develop unhealthy habits. Doctors have advised against taking a smartphone into the bedroom because of the sleep-disrupting impact of screens.

Research has linked excessive Facebook use to low self-esteem and poor life satisfaction. These platforms are addictive, appealing to a desire for self-gratification felt when other users respond to comments or upload content.

Trolls on Twitter have created a toxic environment for women and have been involved in the spreading of misinformation, racism and fake news.

Ease of use, performance and availability

In the UK, over 90% of the population has Internet access. Ofcom, the communications services regulator, has found that the average Briton spends 24 hours per week online. In other countries like Somalia and Eritrea, however, less than 2% of the population has Internet access.

Social media sites are generally very easy to use on a smartphone. For anyone with an Internet connection, they are constantly available, with some people checking their accounts every few minutes. Most people with a social media account check it several times a day.

Accessibility

Social media sites have made great efforts to make their sites accessible to all users, including those with sight, hearing or mobility impairment. Facebook, followed by over 90% of social media users, has a dedicated accessibility team to help both users and staff.

Thirty-two percent of social media users are on Twitter. The platform is used to send short, mostly text-based messages of up to 280 characters long known as a 'tweet'. For people with a disability, it's a good way to get disability-specific information and support causes that affect them.

As Twitter is mostly text-based, it is generally already accessible and there is a team dedicated to addressing any accessibility issues that come up. Third-party apps, such as Twitterific, use software called VoiceOver to navigate the Twitter timeline, compose tweets and attach image descriptions.

Case study: Accessibility on Facebook

To date, Facebook has:

- used facial recognition so that someone using a screen reader would know if their friend was in a photo
- set up keyboard shortcuts to let users go between Help, Home, Profile, Friends, Inbox, Notifications, Account Settings, Privacy and About sections
- launched automated alternative text in an iOS app for English-speaking users. This feature can detect things like the number of people in a photo and their facial expressions, as well as the weather and various objects.

Using social media as a source of news

According to a survey, 41% of social media users use it to stay up-to-date with news and current events. This is of huge concern not only to journalists and newspaper owners, but also to governments who are aware that some social media platforms are being used to micro-target individuals with biased news reinforcing opinions that can be determined by, for example, 'Likes' on Facebook.

In the third quarter of 2018, Twitter lost 9 million of its 335 million users. Its value on the Stock Exchange soared by more than 15%. Why? The loss of users was mainly not down to losing actual users but was due to a purge against "bots" or troll accounts, not belonging to any real person. These are fake accounts created by political enemies or extremists wishing to publicise their cause to willing and susceptible subscribers. By banning troll accounts, Twitter made itself more attractive to advertisers who do not want their products or services promoted on a platform used to spread hate speech, spam and false information.

Newspapers, TV and radio companies are accountable to their readers and listeners – if they make libellous comments, they can be fined or sued. There are no controls over social media posts. Individuals should be extremely wary about believing newsfeeds that they read on social media. The person sitting next to you may be receiving completely different news about the same event, and you will never know that the news you each receive may be simply an echo chamber perpetuating biased views, increasing divisions in society and reducing opportunities for informed discussion.

Case study: Doubling of measles cases

Health experts have warned that a growing anti-vaccine movement in Europe, fuelled by social media and anti-establishment populists, is putting lives at risk and may be to blame for measles outbreaks hitting a 20-year high. There were over 60,000 measles cases in 2018, with 72 deaths, twice as many as in 2017.

Health experts say vaccine sceptics are driving down immunisation rates for measles, flu and other diseases, influenced by posts by social media. The EU's Health Commissioner said, "It is unimaginable that we have children dying of measles. We promised that by 2020 Europe would be measles-free."

Cost

Since social media first began, it has been free for users. It costs nothing to create an account and engage with as many people as you like. This is unlikely to change since if one platform started to charge, users would start to move over to another. The huge profits for social media companies come from advertising.

Hidden costs and privacy

Even though you may not be paying in cash, you are paying in other ways. You are handing over your personal information for free. Facebook knows more about the world population than Google or many governmental organisations; it knows your age, location, birthday, likes, dislikes, networks of friends, and major life events. It even knows when you're happy or sad, and it can tweak the posts you receive based on what it knows about you. Your personal data is valuable and is used by advertisers to target advertisements.

Emojis are used on social media to indicate mood and preferences

Security threats

- Identity thieves can steal your identity – use a strong password. An identity thief who has obtained your email account may click on "Forgot password" on your social media account. They can then gain access to your personal information.

- Be careful with your status updates. Don't post "We're all off on holiday tomorrow… Yippee!" – you could be letting a burglar know the house will be empty for a week. Use privacy controls.

- Be careful not to inadvertently let stalkers find you. The more you post, the more vulnerable you become to those who may wish to harm you. To keep sites from tracking your activity, click on the "Do Not Track" feature.

Exercises

1. Wikipedia is an example of a wiki.

   (a) Describe **two** features of this wiki. [4]

   (b) Describe **two** benefits of the wiki to users of the website. [4]

2. "Over a third of UK 15-year-olds use the internet for six or more hours a day, with much of that time dedicated to social networking sites."

   Discuss the reasons why teenagers spend so much time on social media sites. [6]

3. Gina has an account with several social media sites. She is worried about security and personal privacy issues.

   (a) Describe **two** threats to security when using social media sites. [4]

   (b) Explain **two** measures Gina should take to reduce these threats. [4]

4. Evaluate the implications for individuals of using social media. You should take into account in your evaluation factors such as age group, time spent on sites and the various reasons why individuals use social media. [12]

Chapter 18
Organisations and online communities

Objectives

- Describe the implications for organisations of using and accessing online communities:
  - Employee and customer experience – ease of use, performance, availability, accessibility
  - Customer needs
  - Cost
  - Implementation – timescales, testing
  - Replacement or integration with current systems
  - Productivity
  - Working practices
  - Security

Commercial organisations and social media

According to surveys carried out during 2017-2018, between 70% and 80% of shoppers make buying decisions based on social media. Rather than trust in what the advertisers say, consumers tend to believe what their peers say. They seek their opinions and referrals before buying, and their validation after buying.

Customer needs

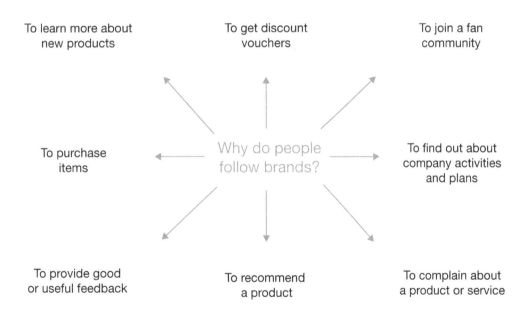

Social media is generally free to users and provides the opportunity to connect with followers every time they log on. If the social posts are entertaining and informative, followers will be pleased to see a particular brand's new content in their feeds, and the brand will be in the forefront of their mind when they are ready to make a purchase.

Organisations using online communities

Why do retailers and organisations offering services need an online presence?

- To share news about new or improved products and services

- To post photographs of customers enjoying their products or facilities, to encourage others to buy or join

- To get customer feedback on their products

- To learn what customers are saying about them so they can address any problems or offer new or improved services and products

- To manage and deal with complaints in a timely way

- To increase website traffic. Sharing content from your website to social media channels encourages visitors to visit the website

Employee and customer experience

Suppose that Joe, the marketing manager at the local gym, has been put in charge of building the company's online presence.

Joe needs to evaluate the groups that the company has joined and focus on the top three to five groups that most accurately reflect the target viewing audience. Each group needs have at least a few hundred members but not more than a few thousand, for maximum visibility.

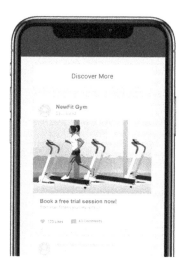

Social media advertisement

Joe needs to ensure that the company proactively visits each of the top groups three or four times a week, or followers will lose interest. Employees and customers can be invited to join discussions and post comments. The group can be promoted on the company website and in email advertising communications.

Participating in social chats is a good way to increase visibility, get attention from potential new customers, display your expertise and drive traffic to the website.

Define the group that this ad is targeting.

Ease of use, availability and accessibility

One of the great advantages of advertising on social media is that it is constantly available, and the great majority of customers are likely to be completely familiar with its use.

An organisation using social media to connect with their customer base can help to make the platforms more accessible by:

- adding captions or alternative text to images
- adding captions to videos
- giving hyperlinks meaningful text so people know where the link goes
- capitalising the first letter of each word in a hashtag to make sure it's read out properly by screen readers.

Cost

There is an overhead cost for an organisation setting up and maintaining an online presence; it is time-consuming, and the organiser or marketing staff have to be paid.

Some large organisations may outsource this function to a social media management agency. This can cost anything from £500 to about £20,000 per month.

Generally, business and organisation accounts are free to set up. The power of a social media platform depends entirely on the strength of its user base; people want to join networks with the most people, or there is less opportunity for interaction. If, for example, Facebook started charging businesses a monthly fee, many would simply leave and go to another platform.

Social media platforms will charge for advertising on their site. There are several variables that can increase or decrease the price of an advertisement on sites such as Facebook, Instagram, Twitter and LinkedIn. These factors include:

- Season, day of the week and the time of day
- How many users are being targeted
- The nature of the organisation – financial organisations may pay a higher price than a small retailer, for example

Costs may be calculated on a cost per click basis, with a charge typically being made for each click on the advertising content, or for each click that takes the user to the organisation's website.

Facebook analytics provide information on reach and engagement

Implementation

An organisation or company planning to develop its online presence needs to be clear about its objectives, and how these can be achieved and measured. For example, the person driving the project should ask:

- Is there someone in the organisation who is familiar or experienced in developing an online presence and marketing through online media?
- What online resources, such as a website with online sales capabilities, do they already have?
- Do they have content such as photographs and videos that would work well online?
- What is the current traffic to the website?

Timescales

Objectives need to be specific, measurable, achievable and realistic. A **timescale** should be set stating a date by which the objectives should be achieved. The organisation needs to be clear about:

- Who they want to connect with
- What content they will share
- How they will interact with people, and how they can influence their actions

Replacement or integration with current systems

Setting up a social media presence is unlikely to cause any issues with integration or replacement of any current marketing systems or strategies. For many companies, it may be more cost-effective than advertising in printed media or sending printed catalogues to everyone on a mailing list. Some organisations may use social media as an additional, rather than a replacement method of marketing.

Working practices, productivity

For an organisation, customers or clients are the most effective consultants they can have. It's important for organisations to listen and understand their wants and needs. An organisation can support customers by setting up forums and other tools to encourage consumers to talk to and support each other.

It is crucial for the organisation to be able to assess the success of their online presence, the size and engagement of their audience. Metrics that can be used include:

- Page likes – how many people have "liked" the page
- Page reach – how many people have seen the page
- People – how many people have clicked on a link sending them to the website
- Return on investment (ROI) – e.g., an increase in sales that can be linked to a particular advertisement

Feedback from customers can motivate employees, inspire new ideas for additional products or services and change working practices.

Ben Grant
September 12 at 12.45 AM   43 min

Attended my first ever (trial) session at NewFit gym at 6am this morning, feeling totally invigorated and a bit sore!! What a fantastic group of people, great times.

♥ Like   💬 Comment

Security

Social media accounts need to be protected. An organisation may, for example, reserve their brand's handle on all social media sites, even if they are not currently using them, so that they will be able to keep a consistent presence across all networks. However, an unmonitored account can be a target for hackers, who can start posting fraudulent messages of their own. They may also post virus-infected links that will pose a threat to followers of the social media site.

Hackers may use a fake profile to connect with an employee of a company and persuade them to share a file that gives them remote access to the company network.

Steps to prevent hacking

- **Use a strong password.** Use a different password for each social media account and change the password regularly, for example every six months to a year.

- **Use two-factor authentication**, which requires the user to provide further evidence that they are the account holder by using something that only they possess, such as a smartphone.

- **Educate all employees** to be vigilant in recognising phishing attacks.

- **Limit the number of people** in the organisation who can post on the social media account. Even though there may be whole teams of people working on social media messaging, content creation or customer service, not everyone needs to know the password or be able to post.

- **Monitor all accounts**, whether they are in daily use or have never been used at all. Someone should be put in charge of this function, and should follow up on any unexpected, inappropriate or negative post. It could be a hacker testing security before creating something more dangerous.

- **Watch for fraudulent sites impersonating your brand**. Set up alerts for brand mentions and check that they are legitimate.

Exercises

1. A private tuition agency has several thousand tutors on its books, covering all school subjects at different levels. Their marketing team uses social media to access online communities.

   (a) Describe **two** different types of online communities they should target. [4]

   (b) Analyse the costs the agency will incur in maintaining a successful social media presence. [10]

2. David is in charge of marketing at a School of Dance. The School runs dance classes for young people from pre-schoolers to students studying for dance exams and qualifications. They also hold Pilates classes for adults.

   David has decided that the School should use social media to increase membership.

   (a) Describe two steps that he should take before committing to this plan. [4]

   (b) Discuss the possible benefits of advertising on social media rather than using newspaper advertisements or leaflets distributed in the town. [8]

   David is concerned that the security of the School's IT systems may be put at risk by using social media.

   (c) Describe **two** possible security risks to the School of having social media accounts. [4]

   (d) Describe **three** methods that can be used to minimise the risk of a security breach. [6]

Protecting data and information

In this section:

Chapter 19
Threats to data

Objectives

- Describe what is meant by: integrity of data, security of data
- Describe the characteristics of threats to data: accidental damage, viruses and other malware, hackers, phishing

Integrity of data

Modern organisations collect and store huge amounts of data, through surveys and questionnaires as well as through the transactions (sales, appointments, client registrations, etc.,) that occur throughout the day. This data is typically used in making top-level management decisions.

A large hospital collects data on all patient admissions, including personal data, length of stay and outcome.

(a) List some management decisions that may be based on an analysis of this data.

(b) Name some other types of organisation that collect data and describe how that data is used.

Data integrity refers to the **accuracy** and **correctness** of data. Organisations need to ensure that procedures are in place to help maintain data integrity during **collection** and **processing**.

Data entry

Manual data entry can result in errors, so proper **training** of staff is essential to ensure they know how to input data accurately, and the importance of doing so. **Auditing procedures** need to be in place so that individuals can be held accountable for inaccurate data entry.

Data validation should be used to ensure the values that the user can enter are restricted. Data validation checks include type checks, range checks, format checks, length checks and presence checks.

Give **one** example of each of these validation checks.

Data verification is the process of entering data twice, with the second entry being automatically checked against the first. If they match, the data is accepted. This is often used when entering and storing a new password.

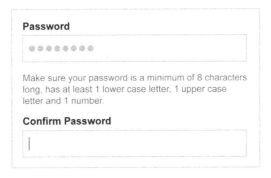

Password

••••••••

Make sure your password is a minimum of 8 characters long, has at least 1 lower case letter, 1 upper case letter and 1 number.

Confirm Password

Verification can also be carried out when entering a customer ID or product code, for example. The system looks up the code in a database and displays the name or description, which can be verified against the expected value printed on an order form.

Processing

Data may be corrupted during processing if a procedure is carried out incorrectly, or there is an error in a program that processes the data. Training in the correct processing of data, and thorough testing of software prior to implementation, are two ways of guarding against this.

Security of data

Keeping data secure means keeping it safe from accidental destruction, and from being stolen, misused or deliberately corrupted or destroyed. Measures include:

- restricting file access to authorised people to reduce the likelihood of accidental corruption or deletion
- having robust backup procedures in place so that data can always be recovered in the event of a disk crash, theft or catastrophic event such as fire or flood

Laptop computers and USB storage devices are particularly susceptible to accidental damage, loss or theft. Often, the data held on a laptop is more valuable than the laptop itself.

Malware

Types of malware include:

- Viruses
- Worms
- Trojan horses ("Trojan")
- Ransomware

Virus

A computer virus is a small piece of software that someone can attach to a host program such as a spreadsheet macro or computer game. Whenever the program is run, the virus program runs too, reproducing itself and attaching to other programs.

Viruses are commonly spread through email attachments, with the email typically inviting the recipient to open a video file, image or joke. The virus can then install and replicate by mailing itself to all the people in the victim's email address book. Their friends may receive an email with an attachment that appears to come from them, which was sent without their knowledge.

Viruses can be used to steal information, harm host computers and networks, create botnets, steal money, and disrupt the host computer's performance. This can be done by corrupting or deleting system files and programs, using up all the computer's memory, reformatting a hard drive or causing frequent computer crashes.

Worm

A **worm** is a standalone malware program that spreads to other computers, often via a network (including the Internet), generally relying on security weaknesses in the host computer to spread itself.

Trojan

The **Trojan** is named after the famous story of the Trojan horse, a huge wooden horse constructed by the Greeks to hide soldiers inside it and trick the Trojans into taking it into the city. Thus, they gained entry to the city of Troy after a fruitless 10-year siege.

The Trojan is malicious software masquerading as a legitimate email that invites the user to open an attachment, which then gives the controller unauthorised access to that computer. It may be used to access personal information such as passwords or banking information. Unlike a virus, Trojans do not normally inject themselves into other software or spread themselves.

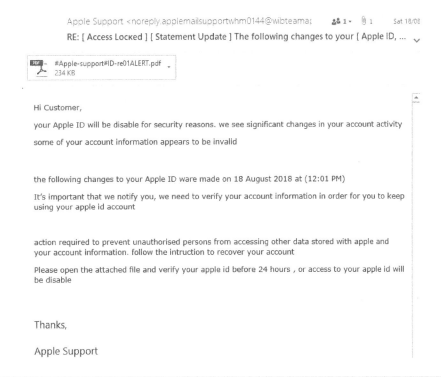

Q3 What clues are there in this email to indicate that is not coming from Apple Inc?

Ransomware attacks

Trojans are often implicated in **ransomware** attacks. By April 2018, about 40% of all malware attacks involved ransomware, targeting individuals and the databases of large organisations. Ransomware is malicious software that, once installed on a computer, denies access to the computer until a ransom is paid. The NHS, universities and numerous commercial organisations suffered serious ransomware attacks in 2018 at the rate of about 38 new attacks every day.

Small and medium-sized companies are frequently targeted because they typically do not have the money to hire cyber-experts, and are more likely to pay the ransom, which often tops £1000 for each infected computer.

Smartphones and mobile devices, increasingly being used for work purposes, are a common target; one security company, Trend Micro, discovered more than 234,000 mobile ransomware apps in 2017. Their research revealed that:

- 83,000 industrial routers were compromised
- 28 industrial robots were infected, allowing the perpetrators to potentially remotely control the robots

 What would be the possible impacts on a company of industrial robots being controlled by a criminal?

Hacker attacks

Hacking is defined as unauthorised access to a computer system. The motivation is typically blackmail or the theft of personal data, which may then be used in identity fraud, enabling the hacker to access bank accounts or make purchases with stolen credit card details.

High-profile cases involving the theft of millions of items of personal data appear regularly in the news.

Denial of service (DOS) attacks

This is an attempt to make a website inaccessible to genuine users or to disrupt services by overloading the website servers and resources with fake traffic.

Case studies

Lloyds Banking Group suffered a DOS attack over two days in January 2017 when Lloyds, Halifax and Bank of Scotland were bombarded with millions of fake requests, designed to bring their computer systems to a grinding halt. A ransom demand, to be paid in the Bitcoin cryptocurrency, was demanded. However, no personal accounts were compromised, and Lloyds paid no ransom before their experts blocked the source of the attacks. Some customers complained that they could not log in while the attack was in progress, but most experienced normal service.

In June 2018, Dixon's Carphone Warehouse was hit by a major cyberattack and compromised nearly six million customer bank card details and more than a million personal data records.

 What are the possible short-term and long-term consequences of attacks such as the ones described?

Phishing

A phishing scam is a fraudulent email or message that appears to come from a legitimate organisation. Its purpose is to trick the recipients into sharing sensitive information such as passwords, usernames, bank and credit card details for malicious purposes. Attackers may make contact via email, social media, phone calls or text messaging.

A phishing email is not personalised, and the same email will be sent out to thousands, or tens of thousands, of people.

Security Update

Please note that starting from Thursday, October 12, 2017 we will be introducing new online banking authentication procedures in order to protect the information of our online banking users.

This is the security information that will be added to your account.

- Two-factor authentication
- Security Question

You are required to confirm your personal details with us as you will not be able access our online service untill this has been done. As you're already registered for online banking all you need to do is to confirm your online banking details.

https://hsbc.com/UpdateSecurity?Token=86NM864576672LWP

Once you've completed this process you will be able to have full access to our online banking service. Your new updated security information will be added to your account within 2 weeks of your account being verified.

Would you click on a link in this email?

Spear-phishing

Unlike phishing attacks, spear-phishing attacks target a specific victim, and messages are modified to include personal information. This makes them much more difficult for a user to identify. The spear-phisher may get their information by viewing personal profiles on social media sites, from which they will be able to find, for example, a person's email address, friends list, geographic location, and posts about new gadgets that were recently purchased or places they have visited.

An attacker posing as a friend may ask for usernames and passwords for various websites so that they can access photos, for example, but having got that password, they will try the same password or variations of it to access confidential information such as credit card details.

Exercises

1. Describe **two** methods that can be used to help ensure that transactional data entered is accurate. [4]
2. Describe **three** ways in which data personal data held by an organisation may be lost or stolen. [6]
3. Westerfield's is a chain of retail stores which holds personal data about tens of thousands of customers on its computer system.

   Analyse the threats to this data and the potential consequences to the company of accidental data loss or a data security breach. [8]

Chapter 20
Impact of threats to data, information and systems

Objectives

- Describe the impact of threats to data, information and systems:
  - on individuals
  - on organisations

Malicious and accidental threats

The consequences of malicious and accidental threats to the security and integrity of data can be very severe, both for individuals and organisations. The last chapter described the various threats to data, both accidental and malicious. This chapter examines some of the consequences for individuals and organisations of these threats.

Impact of threats on individuals

Identity theft

Identity theft can have very serious consequences for an individual. By obtaining access to personal details such as name, address and birthdate, a fraudster can apply for benefits, obtain new credit cards, bank accounts and even mortgages in your name. They may run up thousands of pounds worth of debt in your name, and companies will expect the victim to pay.

It may be extremely stressful and time-consuming to get the situation resolved.

- Identity theft can make victims stressed, anxious, unable to concentrate and have difficulty sleeping

- Identity fraud can also impact employment, housing, insurance, credit status and educational opportunities

Cyberstalking

Cyberstalking is the use of the Internet, email, instant or text messages, or social media posts to stalk or harass a victim.

- Individuals who stalk offline will usually use some form of technology as a tool, e.g. mobile phones, social networks, computers or geolocation tracking

- Cyberstalking is where the perpetrator uses technology but doesn't actually stalk the person in the physical offline world

 Describe the possible impact of cyberstalking on a vulnerable individual.

Spyware is often sold as legitimate employee or child monitoring software. It can also enable a stalker to control the victim's computer, read emails, see passwords and access stored information.

The cyberstalker tricks the victim into opening an email attachment, for example a photograph, and the software is then installed on the PC, unknown to the victim and often undetected by anti-virus software. It can even be used to turn on a device's camera or microphone.

Victims may be harassed, bullied, blackmailed or have malicious gossip spread about them.

Impact of threats on organisations

Phishing attacks

Phishing attacks are often aimed not just at stealing personal information. They are often the means by which other malicious programs, such as ransomware attacks, are delivered. Email attachments are the most common way of delivering malicious programs to a computer or network of computers.

According to statistics:

- 97% of users cannot identify a sophisticated phishing email
- 30% of phishing messages are opened by targeted users, and 12% of those users click on the malicious link.

Large organisations are targeted by phishing attacks more than 1,000 times a month. If a single employee clicks on a malicious link, the security of the company network may be compromised, and the attackers may well gain access to sensitive emails and other documents or information. The consequences can be very severe.

Reputational damage: The publicity around a serious breach can be very damaging to the company. It may be perceived by customers as untrustworthy, and customers may switch their bank account, credit card, phone provider, etc., to another company.

Intellectual property loss: Trade secrets, costly research, formulas and recipes, or customer lists may all be stolen. For a technology or pharmaceutical company, for example, a single design could represent millions of pounds in research costs.

Direct costs: The cost of compensation to individuals who have had their data stolen and who have suffered personal financial losses or other consequences as a result, may run into millions. Fines for violations of the Data Protection Act may be levied by the Information Commissioner's Office as a result of a data breach.

Share value: Such an event may wipe millions of pounds off a company's share value.

List the clues in an email which could make you suspicious that it is a phishing attack.

Hacking attacks

Confidential data may be obtained by criminals by hacking into an organisation's files (possibly following a phishing attack from which they obtain access to user IDs and passwords). A stolen laptop or mobile phone may be hacked if it is not protected by a PIN or biometric method, and passwords may be guessed.

Case study: A Level Maths paper leaked

In June 2018, questions from an A Level Maths paper due to be sat the following day were leaked online. Students reported seeing the paper on sale for £200, with sellers offering the first question free to prove they had it. Around 50,000 students took the exam the following morning, and the Exam Board issued a statement to assure students that they had established processes in place to ensure no students would be disadvantaged.

Students who sat the exam were angry at the Board for allowing such a leak to take place, and concerned that they would have to resit the exam.

Q3 Suggest three ways in which such an occurrence could have happened. Describe the likely impact on the Exam Board, and on the students sitting the exam.

Software problems

Problems with software systems can have very negative effects for both organisations and users, as shown by the case study below.

Case study: TSB upgrade

On Friday 20 April 2018 at 4pm TSB began a long-planned upgrade to their computer system, involving the transfer of records and accounts of its 5.2 million customers to a new system. TSB warned its customers that some services such as online banking would not be available until 6pm on Sunday.

On Sunday, when some customers attempted to log in after 6pm, it became apparent that there were 'issues'. Some people reported that their accounts showed incorrect balances, and others could see accounts belonging to other customers. On Monday, TSB's parent company wrongly published a statement on its website stating that the upgrade had been successfully completed. Customers were posting in large numbers on Twitter that they could not access their accounts. By Tuesday, customers trying to contact the telephone banking team were left on hold for more than an hour.

A week later, many customers were still unable to access their accounts or make payments. TSB announced it would waive £10m in overdraft fees and pay extra interest on current accounts as it attempted to prevent thousands of customers leaving.

The chaos continued for several weeks and by the end of July, issues still remained; 26,000 customers had moved their accounts to another bank and 20,000 new customers joined the bank. Only about 37% of over 135,000 complaints had been dealt with. The boss of TSB said he expected that the bank's services would be back to normal by the first quarter of 2019.

List some of the probable effects of the online banking system failure for the bank.

Exercises

1. Mason works for a small firm of accountants. He comes into work one day, switches on his PC and sees his screen display in large text a notice informing him that his files have been encrypted with a unique key.

(a) State what form of malware has been installed on his computer, and what its purpose is. [2]

(b) Describe the implications of this event to the firm. [6]

(c) Mason reports what has happened to Liam, the Managing Director. Liam discovers that no other computers in the firm have been exposed to the malware.

Describe **three** options available to Liam, and the possible consequences of each action. [6]

2. Describe the possible impact of the theft of personal data held by an organisation on:

(a) individuals whose data is held [6]

(b) the organisation. [6]

Chapter 21
Methods of protecting data

Objectives

Describe:

- the features, characteristics and implications of using antivirus software to protect data
- the process and implications of using passwords for protecting data and systems
- the features, characteristics and implications of using firewalls to protect data

Protecting against viruses

Installing anti-virus software is the first step, for most individuals and organisations, in protecting a computer against malware. Thousands of new viruses are created every day, so it is essential to keep anti-virus software up-to-date. The latest versions of operating systems such as Windows have free anti-virus software included, and this is regularly updated as new viruses are discovered.

Computer scan

Scan your computer
Scan all local disks and clean threats

Custom scan
Select the scan targets, cleaning level and other parameters

Removable media scan
Scanning of USB, DVD, CD and other removable media

Repeat last scan

Functions of anti-virus software

Virus detection

The main function of anti-virus software is to detect and remove computer viruses. Typically, it will scan all the files on your computer and compare them to a database of known virus signatures. This database is updated many times a day in order to ensure that the software will recognise the latest viruses. Most anti-virus software will also scan files in real time so that a virus entering the system is instantly detected. A user can also initiate a scan of selected devices.

Monitoring for system problems

A virus may cause a computer system to behave erratically or slow down, or its memory to fill up. Many anti-virus programs will monitor a computer for signs that a component is not functioning correctly, since this can indicate the presence of a virus. It will then initiate a scan to detect the cause of the problem and if a virus is detected, it will **quarantine** or delete the infected file.

Quarantining a file

Anti-virus software may identify a file as probably, but not definitively, infected by a virus. In that case the file is not deleted immediately but is removed to a separate area of storage. It is not deleted until either the user chooses to delete it, or a pre-set period of time expires. This gives the user the option of removing the file from quarantine and protecting it from future action by the anti-virus software.

Malware removal

Some anti-virus software can also detect and remove other types of malware, such as worms, spyware and Trojans, installed on a computer.

Online security

Some software has features to protect a computer system from other threats such as phishing attacks. It may alert the user to a possible phishing attack, an attempt to redirect a browser or to steal personal information. A warning message may be displayed if a user clicks on a link to download an executable file, which could potentially contain a virus.

PayPal Service <ticket.number7544@cs-webappid.com>
Re: You have added a new email address to your PayPal account

Dear Costumer,

This is a confirmation that you have added a new email address (missy9051@hotmail.com) to your P_a_y_P_a_l account.

If you did not add this email, please get in touch with us. Click Here

You must notify us to help ensure that your account is not accessible to anyone without your knowledge.

Sincerely,
_P_a_y_P_a_l

 What are the signs that this is a phishing attack? Describe the possible consequences to an organisation of an employee clicking on a link in a phishing email.

Keeping operating system software up-to-date

Upgrading software can be an important step in protecting against viruses. Obsolete systems such as Windows XP and Office 2000 are no longer supported and have security weaknesses which can be exploited by hackers.

Organisations and individuals who do not upgrade are putting their systems and data at risk. The latest operating system software will automatically check for security weaknesses as soon as they are recognised and install upgraded software.

Stay up to date – stay secure

Windows 10 makes it easy to keep your PC up to date by automatically checking for the latest updates. You'll get new features and the latest security enhancements to help ensure you're always protected. Best of all, this comes with fewer restarts when you're using your PC the most; simply set your active hours.

 If an organisation has an up-to-date, paid-for, third-party virus checker, why is having an old version of an operating system a security threat? What are the possible consequences?

Passwords

User IDs, PINs and passwords are essential protection against hackers attempting to steal files or personal information. Users in organisations are required to enter their user ID or password in order to access the system. Smartphones and mobile devices require a user to login as soon as they switch on or activate their device.

Choosing a password

There are some basic rules for choosing a strong password and keeping it secure:

- Do not leave a list of passwords in a drawer or write a password on a post-it note stuck on your computer.

- Do not use personal dates or information such as family names or dates of birth, as passwords.

- Do not use a sequence of numbers, such as '12345', or a sequence of letters, such as 'qwerty'.

- Do not use easily guessed words such as your favourite football team or holiday location.

- Do not use the same password for all your accounts.

- Change your passwords regularly.

- Choose an apparently random password comprising at least eight upper- and lower-case letters, numeric and special characters.

Your password must have:
- 8 or more characters
- Upper & lowercase letters
- At least one number

Strength: strong

Avoid passwords that are easy to guess or used with other websites.

Firewall

A firewall refers to a network device which blocks certain kinds of network traffic, forming a barrier between a trusted and an untrusted network such as the Internet. It can be implemented as hardware, software, or a combination of both.

It is considered to be the first line of defence in preventing unauthorised access to or from a private network, or even a standalone computer. Most home routers have a built-in firewall which can protect Internet-borne attacks. The router can also stop an infected computer from attacking other computers by preventing malicious software from leaving your network.

How a firewall works

The firewall filters information coming through an Internet connection into a private network or computer system. Numbered doors called **ports** are opened so that only certain traffic is allowed to pass through.

Some operating systems have a built-in firewall. Windows 10 has a **one-way firewall** that protects a system from incoming threats. A **two-way firewall** will also prevent malware or undesired applications from connecting to the Internet. Some organisations use firewalls to prevent employees sending certain types of email or transmitting sensitive data outside of the network.

Configuring a firewall

In an organisation using a private network, the network manager can specify the firewall configuration. The rules defining access can help to ensure that genuine users can access a website, while hackers cannot access server management or internal databases. By restricting unauthorised processes, firewalls prevent the spread of malicious computer viruses, worms and trojans that may attempt to install or hijack the application, hardware or network.

 An employee working on a PC at home uses the Internet regularly. Should they install a firewall to help prevent malware attacks? Is a firewall software, or a hardware device?

Limitations of a firewall

A firewall cannot protect against insider attack, nor can it protect against malware introduced via a flash drive or other portable device.

It also cannot protect against a "backdoor" attack; a malware type that bypasses normal authentication procedures and security checks.

If it is not properly configured, a firewall can give a false impression that the network is safe.

Exercises

1. (a) The Computer Centre manager in a firm of financial consultants has set new rules for user passwords.

    • The password must be at least 10 characters long.

    • It must not be a name or word in the dictionary.

    Give **two** more rules that could be added to ensure that a password is very unlikely to be discovered by a hacker. [2]

    (b) Explain how anti-virus software works. [6]

2. Mark is responsible for the network and system security at a college.

    (a) A firewall is used to protect the system from unauthorised access from outside the network. Describe how the firewall does this. [3]

    (b) State **three** limitations of a firewall. [3]

    (c) The operating system at the college was installed some years ago and Mark is concerned that it poses a security risk.

    Describe **two** reasons why the operating system may compromise the security of the college network. [4]

3. Susan is responsible for data security in a company manufacturing sophisticated military defence equipment. The network is protected by a firewall, and anti-malware software. She is concerned, however, that a successful phishing attack could compromise network security and lead to hackers gaining access to sensitive data. She is considering the purchase of specific anti-phishing software.

    Discuss the issues she should consider before purchasing the software. [8]

Chapter 22
Encryption, protocols and digital certificates

Objectives

- Describe the features, applications and implications of encryption methods used to protect:
  - data during transmission
  - stored data
- Describe the processes and techniques of protecting data and systems:
  - digital certificates
  - protocols

Encryption

Encryption is the encoding of data so that it cannot be read directly.

- Plaintext: the original message to be encrypted
- Ciphertext: the encrypted message
- Encryption: the process of converting plaintext into ciphertext
- Key: a piece of information or a random string of bits used for scrambling and unscrambling data
- Encryption algorithm: the formula for encrypting the plaintext

The Caesar cipher, said to have been used by Julius Caesar in Ancient Roman times, is a very simple encryption method, called a substitution cipher, in which each letter is replaced by another letter further along the alphabet.

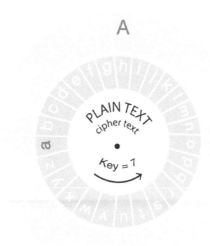

A Caesar cipher wheel

(a) Using a key of 3, use the cipher to encrypt the name **KEN.**

(b) Using a key of 7, decrypt the word **flz.**

Symmetric encryption

The Caesar cipher is a very simple example of **symmetric encryption**. In this type of encryption, the same key is used to both encrypt and decrypt the data. Of course, the Caesar cipher would never be used in reality, but there are many other more complex algorithms that may be used in symmetric encryption.

However, its great weakness is that if the key is discovered by a hacker, the hacker can decrypt messages without this being detected by either the sender or the receiver.

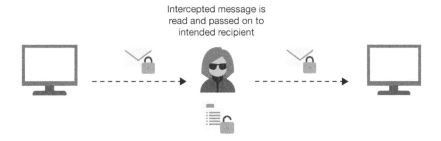

Symmetric encryption is not secure from hackers

Symmetric encryption is also known as **private key encryption** because the key is theoretically only known to the sender and recipient.

Asymmetric encryption

Also known as **end-to-end encryption**, this is a much more secure technique. There are two keys:

- The **public key**, available to anyone who wishes to send an encrypted message to the recipient (e.g. a bank)

- The **private key**, available only to the recipient, which is used to decrypt the message

The keys are numbers which have been paired together. Key 1 (the public key) is made up of two very large prime numbers paired together. Key 2 is one of these prime numbers. The larger the public key number, the more difficult it is to find the other prime factor needed to break the code.

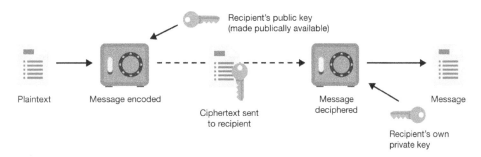

Asymmetric encryption

Strong and weak encryption

The largest known prime number is $2^{82,589,933} - 1$, with 24,862,048 digits. A 300-digit number with just two prime factors would take an estimated 150,000 years for a powerful computer to crack.

Encryption is considered "strong" when the useful lifetime of the encrypted data is less than the time taken to break the code.

Some governments have banned encryption above a certain strength because they do not want dissidents or terrorists to be able to communicate without being able to intercept and decrypt their communications. However, widely used apps such as WhatsApp (owned by Facebook), a messenger service for smartphones which uses the Internet to send messages, images, audio or video, now use strong encryption. WhatsApp has a billion users worldwide.

Case study: The Enigma cipher

The Enigma cipher is one of the most famous ciphers of the twentieth century. It was used by the Germans during World War II to encrypt communications to and from the German Navy, Army and Air Force. Messages were encrypted and decrypted using the Enigma machine, which looked something like an old-fashioned typewriter.

The code settings were changed daily, and the Germans were convinced that the code could never be broken. However, with the help of a reconstructed Enigma machine, code-breakers at Bletchley Park managed to crack the code. This enabled the British Intelligence Services to track German plans and movements, which some experts think shortened the war by as many as two to four years.

Protecting stored data

Many organisations hold huge amounts of personal information about employees and customers, which by law must be protected from loss or theft. Intellectual property, recipes, formulae, research papers and results, may also need to be kept completely secure. The recipe for Coca-Cola remains a closely guarded secret more than 130 years after it was invented.

Increased use of laptops and other mobile devices poses an increased risk to data, since these devices may be more easily lost or stolen than PCs in an office.

Utility software is readily available which will encrypt every section of a hard drive or external storage device, preventing unauthorised access to anyone accessing the files without permission.

Data on smartphones may be encrypted by applying security settings. A passcode is then needed to unlock and read the data.

Protecting data during transmission

Protocols

A protocol is a set of rules relating to communication between devices. In order to allow equipment from different suppliers to be networked, a standardised set of rules (protocols) has been devised covering standards for physical connections, cabling, mode of transmission, speed, data format, error detection and correction. Any devices which use the same communications protocol can be linked together.

HTTP (Hypertext Transfer Protocol) is the standard protocol used to access and receive web pages in the form of HTML (Hypertext Markup Language) files on the Internet.

Secure link

HTTPS (Hypertext Transfer Protocol Secure) is used to secure data transmitted between a user and a website.

SSL (Secure Sockets Layer) is used to establish an encrypted link between a web server and a user. It is the industry standard security technology, used by millions of websites, to ensure that communications and online transactions with their customers cannot be intercepted.

In order to create an SSL connection, a web server requires an **SSL certificate**. An IT manager wishing to activate SSL on their web server will be prompted to answer a number of questions about the identity of the website and the organisation. The web server then creates the two keys needed for **public key encryption**, the public key and the private key.

The website address will then start with the letters **https://** and display a padlock icon. If a user clicks on the padlock icon, information about the SSL certificate will be displayed.

Typically, an SSL certificate will contain the domain name, company name, address and country. It will also contain the expiration date of the certificate and details of the Certification Authority responsible for the issuance of the certificate. The diagram below shows how https works.

1. User requests secure SSL connection from Website host

3. Secure connection is now established

2. Host responds with valid SSL certificate

When a browser connects to a secure site, it will retrieve the site's SSL Certificate and check that it has not expired, that it has been issued by a Certification Authority the browser trusts, and that it is being used by the website for which it has been issued. If it fails any of these checks, the browser will display a warning to the end user letting them know that there is a problem with the website's security certificate and the site is not secure.

Transport Layer Security (TLS) is the successor to Secure Sockets Layer (SSL) and performs a similar function, enabling secure communication over the Internet.

An SSL or TLS certificate used by a secure HTTPS website is an example of a **digital certificate**. Digital certificates are also used by companies that frequently need documents such as contracts, agreements or applications to be signed. They are issued by Certificate authorities who first of all verify the identity of the applicant.

A digital certificate can be attached to a password-protected, encrypted email message or data file. Its most common use is to verify that a user sending a message is who they claim to be, and to provide the recipient with the means to send an encoded reply

Digitally signed documents offer many added benefits:

- similar legal integrity as physically signed documents
- ability to lock down the document against future edits
- timestamps
- reduced turnaround time
- no postage costs
- less wasted paper

 Suggest some organisations that frequently need documents signed by their customers.

Wireless security standards

The most common wireless security standards are:

- WEP (Wired Equivalent Privacy) and
- WPA (Wi-Fi Protected Access)

In addition to preventing access by a hacker to a particular network, these security protocols also encrypt data to prevent it from being understood if it is hacked during transmission. WPAv2 is the latest and most secure standard for wireless transmission.

Exercises

1. (a) (i) Describe what is meant by an **Internet protocol**. [2]

    (ii) State why Internet protocols are necessary. [1]

    (iii) Name a standard Internet protocol used to access and receive web pages. [1]

    (b) State **three** items that may be specified in a protocol. [3]

2. Amir works for YourHome, a letting agency that rents out properties. YourHome owns a digital certificate in order to securely sign, send and store documents in the cloud. Documents that require digital signatures include landlord contracts, tenancy agreements, references, property advertisements and inventories.

    (a) Explain reasons why YourHome uses a digital certificate instead of posting documents to be signed and returned by customers. [6]

    (b) Describe how a digital certificate ensures that communication over the Internet is secure. [4]

    (c) Amir logs on to a website which uses the https protocol. A message pops up: "Your connection is not private".

    State **two** reasons why this may occur. [2]

Chapter 23
Role of legislation in protecting data

Objectives

Describe:

- the role of current legislation in protecting data and IT systems from attack and misuse

- the impact on individuals and organisations of legislation designed to protect data and IT systems

- the purpose, role and impact, on individuals and organisations, of codes of practice for the protection of data produced by the Information Commissioner's Office and professional bodies

The need to protect data

All organisations hold personal data about their employees, customers or clients. Think of some of the organisations that you belong to or have dealings with: your school, doctor's surgery, sports club, retailers or travel companies. Your data needs to be protected from being stolen and misused.

Case study: BA faces £500m fine for data breach

In September 2018, British Airways admitted that 380,000 customers' bank details could have been stolen from its website and smartphone app. Hackers stole names, email addresses and credit card details - including the long number, expiry date and the three-digit CVV security code.

The breach lasted two weeks before it was noticed by the airline, and some customers complained they were not notified until more than eight hours after the breach was made public. One customer said he had lost almost £1000 to hackers during the breach, and all customers were advised to cancel their bank or credit cards.

A cyber-security researcher claimed to have discovered evidence of a "skimming" script designed to steal financial data from online payment forms. Hacks like this make use of an increasingly common phenomenon, in which large websites embed multiple pieces of code from other sources or third-party suppliers.

Such code may be needed to do specific jobs, such as authorise a payment or present ads to the user. But malicious code can be slipped in instead - this is known as a supply chain attack. RiskIQ said the malicious script consisted of just 22 lines of code. It worked by grabbing data from BA's online payment form and then sending it to the hackers' server once a customer hit the "submit" button.

Under the new Data Protection Act 2018, companies can be fined up to £17 million or 4% of global turnover, whichever is bigger. Previously, the maximum fine was £500,000.

 What was the likely impact on British Airways of the data breach, in addition to a substantial fine?

The General Data Protection Regulation (GDPR)

This applies to all companies based in the EU and those with EU citizens as customers. Non-EU countries are also affected, so inside or outside Europe, the UK would still need to comply with the GDPR. The GDPR forms a part of the **Data Protection Act 2018**.
The GDPR came into effect throughout the European Union in May 2018.

The Data Protection Act 2018

The Act requires organisations that handle personal data to evaluate the risks of processing such data and to implement appropriate measures to mitigate those risks. For many organisations such measures include effective cyber security controls.

The GDPR sets out seven **key principles**:

- Lawfulness, fairness and transparency
- Purpose limitation
- Data minimisation
- Accuracy
- Storage limitation
- Integrity and confidentiality (security)
- Accountability

The Accountability principle is new. This specifically requires organisations to take responsibility for complying with the principles, and to have appropriate processes and records in place to demonstrate that they comply.

The individual's rights of access to their personal data under the GDPR are listed in Learning Aim F, Chapter 32.

Importance of these principles

The GDPR does not give hard and fast rules for data protection, but the principles embody the spirit of the general data protection regime, as stated by the Information Commissioner's Office (ICO): "Compliance with the spirit of these key principles is a fundamental building block for good data protection practice."

What is personal data?

Personal data means any information relating to an identified or identifiable person. This includes, for example, your name, telephone number, address and e-mail address. Personal data may be collected about you directly when you open an account, sign up to receive a newsletter or purchase a product online.

Personal data may also be collected when you visit a website. This type of information may include your type of browser or device, details of the web pages you have viewed, links you clicked on, your IP address, sites clicked on before coming to the current website and any other information you choose to share when using the "Like" functionality on Facebook or the '+1' functionality on Google.

Cookies

Legislation also enforces transparency in online data collection. Consumer data is crucially important to many organisations, but it is important for everyone browsing a website, or using their mobile phone, to know what data is being collected about them. By law, a website must display a message stating that they use cookies to collect personal information. Most websites give the user the option of refusing to allow cookies to gather information.

However the information is collected, the organisation that collects it is legally responsible for keeping it secure.

Impact of legislation on organisations

Most organisations holding personal data must register with the Information Commissioner's Office.

- They must carry out a Data Protection Impact Assessment (DPIA) to identify, assess and minimise privacy risks associated with data processing activities.

- Failure to do so may result in a large fine.

Organisations may appoint a Data Protection Officer whose responsibility is to ensure that appropriate technical and organisational measures are taken for collecting, holding and using data. This includes keeping it secure. This person may be held personally responsible for any breaches and could face a fine or even imprisonment if the organisation does not comply with Data Protection legislation.

Impact of legislation on individuals

For individuals outside the organisation, the legislation means that some personal data which may be held about them cannot be divulged without their permission.

This includes:

- Health, sexual life
- Religious beliefs
- Political opinions
- Racial background
- Trade union membership
- Criminal offences

Codes of Practice

The Information Commissioner's Office (ICO) publishes guidance to help organisations apply Data Protection effectively.

The following advice is given:

- The GDPR recommends that an organisation uses an approved code of conduct to help it to apply the Act effectively.

- Trade associations or bodies representing a sector can create codes of conduct to help their sector comply with the GDPR in an efficient and cost-effective way. They can amend or extend existing codes to comply with GDPR requirements. They have to submit the draft code to the ICO for approval.

Professional bodies

Professional bodies such as the British Medical Society, Law Society and Association of Teachers and Lecturers further the interests of people in a particular profession. Many professional bodies are involved in the development and monitoring of professional educational programs, and the updating of skills.

The British Computer Society (BCS) is a professional body representing those working in Information Technology. It was founded in 1957 and has played an important role in educating and nurturing IT professionals, upholding the profession and creating a global community active in promoting and furthering the field and practice of computing.

The BCS publishes a Code of Practice for IT professionals, with advice and qualifications available on the subject of Data Protection.

The **Data Protection Network** is another professional body which produces practical guides to implementing Data Protection legislation. They suggest that the impact for organisations will include:

- **Preparation for data breaches**
  A data breach plan needs to document instructions for notifying a supervisory authority within 72 hours, ensuring a quick, efficient assessment of what has happened, how to assess the risk and notify customers.

- **Training**
  Staff need to understand the key principles of data protection and avoid putting the organisation at risk.

Impact of codes of practice on organisations

A well thought out code of practice is a major step in ensuring that an organisation has studied and understands the Data Protection Law and has a comprehensive plan for implementing it.

- It may improve standards by establishing best practice
- It may give a competitive advantage
- It may mitigate against enforcement action and reduce the risk of a fine
- It may demonstrate that appropriate safeguards are in place to transfer data to countries outside the UK

Impact of codes of practice on individuals

The code of practice followed by an organisation should ensure that an individual's data is properly protected and that the rights of the individual regarding their data are understood and will be respected.

 Look up the BCS Code of Practice for IT professionals and list the practices it recommends.

The Computer Misuse Act 1990

This Act makes illegal:

- unauthorised access to computer material
- unauthorised access with intent to commit or facilitate further offences
- unauthorised modification of computer material or impairment of operations
- making, supplying or obtaining anything which can be used in computer misuse offences

Hacking, phishing attacks, ransomware attacks and spreading malware are all offences under this law.

While legislation cannot prevent attacks, it can act as a deterrent. However, it can often be very difficult to find the criminals responsible for large-scale attacks and bring them to justice. New forms of attack are regularly perpetrated, and legislation has to keep pace in defining these as illegal and allowing the imposition of appropriate penalties.

The **Police and Justice Act 2006** contained some amendments to the Computer Misuse Act to make Denial of Service attacks illegal, with a maximum penalty of 10 years in jail.

Copyright, Designs and Patents Act 1988

This Act gives the creators of literary, dramatic, musical and artistic works the right to control the ways in which their material may be used. It also applies to computer programs.

The Copyright (Computer Programs) Regulations 1992 extended the Copyright Act, making infringement of copyright both a civil and a criminal offence.

Board directors can be prosecuted for permitting the illegal copying of software or its use in their company.

Exercises

1. Worldwide Adventures is a travel company which organises holiday adventures and experiences in several countries around the world. After being alerted to a possible data breach, the data controller called in cyber-security experts to identify the cause. The experts estimated that the data breach had occurred four months previously and the breach was ongoing.

    (a) Describe **two** actions that the company should take immediately. [4]

    (b) Describe **three** possible impacts on the company of the data breach. [6]

    (c) Describe **two** possible consequences to individuals of the data breach. [4]

2. YourHealth is a private company which offers health assessments, identifying health concerns and giving advice on how to address them. They hold personal data about each of their customers, including data about their medical conditions and the actions which they have been advised to take.

    (a) Assess the role of current legislation in protecting this data from misuse. [8]

    The company follows a Code of Practice for the protection of data, published by the Information Commissioner's Office.

    (b) Describe the purpose of the Code of Practice. [4]

Chapter 24
Access control, backup and recovery

Objectives

- Describe physical access control techniques for protecting data and systems
- Describe the processes and implications of techniques and procedures used in protecting data and systems:
  - file permissions
  - access levels
  - backup and recovery procedures

Purpose of access control

Computer systems and data need to be protected from access by unauthorised individuals, either in person or via electronic means. In this chapter we first consider means of controlling physical access to areas of a building containing computer systems or sensitive information.

- Access controls should identify and allow access only to authorised individuals.
- Some forms of access control may allow access to a room only at specific times of day.
- Some access systems will record the ID and time of everyone entering a building or secure area.

Types of authentication

There are three types of authentication:

- Something the user knows, such as a PIN or password
- Something the user has, such as a smart card or electronic key fob
- A user's physical (biometric) attribute, such as their face, retinal pattern, fingerprint or voice

Door security device

Biometric security measures

A retinal scan, fingerprint scan, face scan or voice recognition can all be used to identify an individual.

Initially, a scan or recording of the individual characteristic is performed, and the digitised pattern stored in the computer system.

When the person attempts to gain entry, the security device performs a scan and compares it with the one stored on the system. If it matches, they are allowed in.

Advantages of biometrics

- Security – biometric methods are almost impossible to hack
- Convenience – PINs and passwords may be forgotten
- Information collected – an organisation can keep track of thousands of employees with one biometric device and software
- Time-saving – it is usually a faster method of gaining access to a device or an area than typing in a PIN or password

Disadvantages of biometrics

- Errors sometimes occur and the biometric device does not recognise the individual
- Clothing, glasses, injury or darkness can affect recognition
- Biometric devices cost more than traditional security devices
- They can be slow if the software has trouble identifying an individual

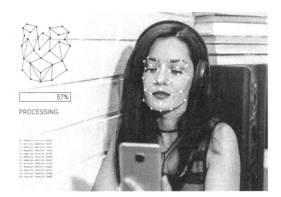

Describe how face recognition may be used to secure a mobile phone.

Describe one other application, apart from security, which may use facial recognition.

File permissions

In a network, files are held on the file server and accessible from all computers in the network. Access to the network is determined initially by the user's login. However, having determined that a valid user has logged on, file permissions may be defined for individual files to control what users can do to the file. File permissions are used to protect data from being deliberately or accidentally amended or deleted.

Each file or folder in a shared area can have rights and permissions assigned to a user group. A user who creates a file in their own area can set file permissions for that file, controlled by a password which they choose.

File permissions may be:

- **read only** – users can access the files and read the contents. The password set by the file's creator must be entered before the contents can be changed or deleted.

- **read/write** – users can access the files and add to contents. They will not be able to delete the files without entering the password. They may be able to copy the files.

- **full access/full control** – users can access the files, edit contents and delete files. No password is required.

Protect Document
Control what types of changes people can make to this document.

Protecting a Word document

Access levels

Access levels are set so that users of a computer system have access only to the applications and data that they need in order to do their jobs. A system administrator can set up a hierarchy of users, whereby low-level users have access to only a limited amount of information. The highest-level users can access all data in the system. Senior managers will have access to more data and applications than junior employees, or employees in a particular department. The Chief Executive may have access to all applications and data.
In a school, students will have access to a personal area that other students will not be able to access.

Backup

Backup of data is essential to ensure that information can still be accessed after an emergency or a disruption of the network or a system.
Some organisations such as banks or airlines cannot afford to lose a single transaction. All transactions are written simultaneously to multiple computer systems in different locations. If one system goes down or suffers a natural disaster, one of the backup systems automatically takes over control.
All organisations need to have backup systems in place, and if they hold personal data, it is a legal requirement to keep data safe and secure.

Case study

A small business selling a range of decorative kitchen equipment online uses an accounting package, held on one of the PCs in their local area network, to record details of all its customers, suppliers, products and transactions. They keep a backup of all their customised layouts for order forms, invoices and statements on Microsoft OneDrive, separately from daily transactional data. The Accounts manager takes a backup before running accounting processes such as creating a VAT return or running year end accounts.

Every night, a scheduled backup takes place, backing up data into a folder on Microsoft OneDrive. The PC holding the data is kept switched on in order for this to be done.

 Give reasons why they hold a backup of their customised form layout in a different folder from the daily backups of files holding details of customers, suppliers, products and transactions.

Recovery procedures

The consequences of data loss following on from a natural or man-made disaster can be extremely severe. Statistics reveal that more than 90% of companies suffering a catastrophic data loss never recover and go out of business within a year.

A disaster recovery plan documents the procedures to be followed in the event of a disaster. Its major objective is to minimise disruption and data loss. The plan should specify:

- the objective and purpose of the plan
- who will be responsible for implementing the plan in the event of disaster
- what procedures will be followed

The benefits of having a documented disaster recovery plan include:

- minimising risk of delays
- guaranteeing reliability of standby systems
- providing a standard for testing the plan
- minimising decision-making during a disaster
- reducing potential legal liabilities
- lowering stress in a potentially very stressful situation

Implications of data loss

Even if data can be recovered after a disaster, there is likely to be considerable disruption. Paper records, manuals and correspondence may be destroyed, hardware may need to be replaced, and all software settings reconfigured. New premises may have to be found, at least temporarily. Considerable time will be spent on restoring systems to their state before any disaster occurred.

Restoring files from backup

There are two types of backup that may be used in an organisation:

- Full backup of all data, which can be restored independently of any other backup. This takes more time and disk space, but restoring files in the event of data loss is a relatively simple process.

- Incremental backup, which records only the changes made since the last backup. This is faster, but restoring files is a more complex procedure. A full backup is made less frequently, for example once a week, say on Monday evening. If a disaster occurs on Friday morning, the incremental backups made on Tuesday, Wednesday and Thursday are applied to the full backup to restore the system to its state on Thursday evening.

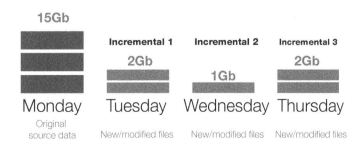

Restoring files from a full backup is much simpler as the entire contents of the backup disk can be copied over to a new hard disk. Special recovery software can be used to repair data files, databases, storage media and corrupted partitions on a hard disk.

In some cases, a specialised data recovery expert may be needed to help recover lost data.

Exercises

1. Elsa is the Managing Director of an advertising agency. She wants to install an access control system at the entrance to the computer centre. She is undecided whether to use a biometric or non-biometric system.

    (a) Describe how **one** method of biometric access control works. [4]

    (b) Discuss the use of biometric and non-biometric methods of access control, giving advantages and disadvantages of each. [8]

2. A school has a computer network used by teaching staff, administrative staff and students.

    (a) Describe what is meant by each of the following terms:

    (i) File permissions [4]

    (ii) Access levels [4]

    (b) Describe how file permissions and access levels may be used by different users in this school environment. [6]

3. Max owns a small company making traditional ice cream, which is sold to farm shops, supermarkets and restaurants. He has a networked computer system on which all the company software and data are held.

    Max has never experienced a system failure or serious data loss, but he is aware that should disaster such as fire or flood strike, he will be ill-prepared to continue in business. He decides that he needs a disaster recovery plan.

    (a) Describe the purpose of a disaster recovery plan. [4]

    (b) Describe **two** topics that are likely to be covered in a disaster plan. [4]

    (c) Describe **one** backup strategy that the company could use to ensure that in the event of disaster, all data could be recovered. [4]

Impact of IT systems

In this section:

Chapter 25
Online services

Objectives

- Describe the features and implications of using online services to support:
  - retail
  - financial services
  - education and training
  - news and information
  - entertainment and leisure
  - productivity
  - booking systems

- Analyse and describe the uses, impacts and implications for individuals and organisations of:
  - transactional data
  - targeted marketing
  - collaborative working

Online retail trade

The online share of retail trade is increasing year on year, with the UK leading the trend worldwide. In 2017 in the UK, online sales accounted for an estimated 17.8% of all retail trade, amounting to almost £70 billion.

 Have you made any online purchases in the past few weeks? What did you buy? Why did you use an online retailer?

Advantages to the consumer of online retail

There are many advantages for customers buying online. Someone living in a remote location, with mobility problems or with no time for shopping, can satisfy almost all of their need for consumer goods by ordering online.

Delivering online orders

- Many supermarkets offer online ordering and delivery. After the first few orders, the order form prioritises items that a customer regularly purchases. Special offers and vouchers are frequently offered, and delivery is swift and efficient.

- Computer equipment, books, toys, clothes, household equipment and thousands of other items can be ordered online at the click of a button, and are often less expensive than a high street store.

- Items such as software are no longer supplied on CDs. As soon as an order is placed the software will become available as a download from the software distributor.

Think of three other advantages for the customer of purchasing goods online.

Advantages to the seller of online retail

A retailer who accepts orders online does not need a physical outlet with staff and a large stock which may never be sold. There is no expensive rent or rates to be paid for a store in a prime location. A warehouse can be located in any convenient place, will need far fewer staff and space per item, and can hold a much larger range of items. Companies such as Amazon have massive warehouses and completely automated systems for accepting orders, order fulfilment, delivery, stock control and all other functions. This means they can offer goods at a cheaper price.

Automatic picking and packing in a warehouse

New retail opportunities

Anyone can buy and sell goods online, for example using eBay.

Have you ever bought or sold goods online? Some individuals make a career out of buying and selling new and second-hand goods online.

Look up the resource: 'Beginners-Guide-to-Buying-and-Selling-on-eBay' on the Internet.

List the advantages and the pitfalls to buyers and sellers.

Implications of online retail services

Online retailing has changed the face of the high street. More and more large, prestigious chains such as John Lewis and Marks & Spencer are having to close stores. Small, specialised shops such as bookshops and boutique clothing stores cannot compete with online prices and are being replaced on the High Street by charity shops, coffee shops and 'Closed' signs.

Case study: Marks and Spencer to close 100 stores by 2022

Of the 100 stores, 21 were shut by June 2018. M&S wants to move a third of its sales online and plans to have fewer, larger clothing and homeware stores in better locations.

The company has just over 1,000 UK stores. The closures in the first half of 2018 affected a total of 872 employees.

"M&S is repositioning itself for the new retail world," said Laith Khalaf, senior analyst at stockbrokers Hargreaves Lansdown. *"Having a huge store estate is no longer the powerful retail force that it once was."*

Online financial services

Financial services include a wide range of businesses that manage money. This includes banks, credit card companies, insurance companies, stock brokerages and many others.

All banks now have an online presence and more than one in four UK bank branches closed between 2013 and 2017. More than 500 are set to go in 2018. Customers increasingly use the Internet and smartphones for day-to-day banking. Cash is used less and less frequently, and when needed can be obtained from ATMs or by using a debit card for cashback in many stores.

 What adverse effects might the closure of banks have? Who would be mainly affected?

Some people do not like using credit or debit cards. They prefer to pay using cash or cheques. Paying in a cheque has traditionally meant that it must be posted or taken to a bank. However, in 2018, Lloyds Bank made it possible to pay in cheques via an app installed on a mobile device.

PayPal is a growing financial service used by millions to make online payments and money transfers.

 Give reasons why some people do not like to use card payments. What are the implications of not using credit or debit card payments at all?

Education and training

More and more education and training is taking place online. Many publishers offer online resources in all school subjects. Google Docs, Google's browser-based word processor, is a free alternative to Microsoft Word that allows students to create, edit, and share documents online and access them from any computer with an Internet connection.

At University level, the Open University offers degree courses for which assignments and tests are completed and submitted online. MOOCs (Massive Open Online Courses) are offered by many universities. A MOOC is a free, interactive step-by-step course aimed at reaching an unlimited number of participants worldwide.

Free online training courses are available for hundreds of programming languages and software packages. If you want to learn how to write an Android app, for example, you can take a free course using the Android Visualiser, which shows you how each line of code you type will look on a smartphone.

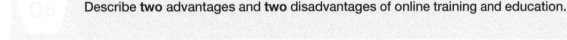

The Android visualiser

Describe **two** advantages and **two** disadvantages of online training and education.

Online news and information

Newspapers are suffering financially. Almost every country in the world is noting a major fall in the print circulation of its newspapers. Most newspapers have experienced a drop in circulation of between 30 and 35% in the last decade, and that is having a serious effect on advertising revenue, which is a crucial element in balancing the books.

Instead, many people are getting their daily news from social media sites such as Facebook and Twitter. About two-thirds of the population, according to some surveys, get at least some of their news from social media platforms. News and issues which are shared on social platforms are reaching large audiences, and are able to impact public opinion and importantly, voter behaviour.

Users are more likely to comment on negative, divisive news stories, and this can create divisions in society. Moreover, the news is often inaccurate and targeted at individual users, designed to fuel prejudices and spread fake news. (See Learning Aim F, Chapter 30.)

Entertainment and leisure

Online entertainment has become ubiquitous. We can pay a subscription to Netflix, Amazon Prime Video or other streaming services and watch TV series, movies, documentaries and more whenever we want to, on any device from a mobile phone to a TV. We can listen to almost any piece of music on a service such as Spotify. Thousands of computer games, free and paid for, can be downloaded to a mobile phone, desktop PC or other device, generating billions of pounds in revenue.

Virtual reality rides such as Galactica at Alton Towers are another aspect of computers used in the leisure and entertainment world. This ride combines the experience of an actual roller-coaster ride with the virtual reality of a ride through space viewed through a headset.

Online entertainment and gaming, however, can have negative consequences. Unsuitable films and other content may be downloaded and watched, games may become addictive.

Case study: Fortnite

Online gaming is a huge growth industry. The third-person shooter game *Fortnite*, released in 2017, quickly became the most popular video game in the world. It can be played or watched on a TV screen with a PlayStation console, on a PC, Mac, Xbox, PS4 or mobile devices. At times, there are more than three million people playing it worldwide. Crucially, it is free, with payment required only for additional features, and by the end of 2018 it had been downloaded an estimated six million times.

But what of the downsides? Parents of teenagers speak of it as an addiction, with the game being played under the desk at school or in the bathroom at 4am. Addicted gamers may neglect schoolwork, leading to plunging grades. Social isolation and neglect of personal relationships may follow. Few people want to be around people who only ever talk about their game of choice. And the more difficulty a person has making friends and maintaining relationships, the more he or she may retreat into their online world.

Physical consequences of gaming addiction include migraines, sleep disturbances, backache, eating irregularities, and poor personal hygiene.

Productivity in the office

Technology has, over the past 20 years, changed workplaces beyond recognition. Hundreds of thousands of jobs have disappeared, but equally, innumerable new opportunities and ways of working have been created. Technology has changed and simplified the ways in which people work.

- Employees can easily collaborate on different projects, work from home or on the train whilst commuting to work.

- Computer systems can ensure that employers have all the information on hand that they need to make the best business decisions.

- Employees can more easily contribute new ideas or solutions to problems even if they are working at remote locations.

- Work flow is improved through the use of planning or scheduling software which allows a project to be recorded and tracked through different stages, managed by different people.

Productivity in manufacturing

Aided by the latest computer equipment and software, artificial intelligence and robotics, mass-production of thousands of items from cars to chemicals, household items, toys and clothes has been revolutionised. However, since 2008, there has been very little manufacturing productivity growth, and evidence suggests that companies with better management are more likely to have higher rates of productivity growth.

In all areas of manufacturing, good decision-making and training of employees, as well as capital investment in the latest manufacturing technology, are likely to boost productivity and profits.

Booking systems

Online booking systems have become the norm. Whether you are booking a cinema ticket, meal at a restaurant, train ticket, flight, hair appointment, or any other of a myriad of activities, it can be done online. Digital tickets or boarding passes, for example, can be downloaded to a mobile phone for valid entry.

 What online booking systems have you or your family used recently? What are the advantages of the online booking system, to the customer and the service provider?

Uses, impacts and implications of online services

Transactional data

Transactional data is information that records an exchange, agreement or transfer (usually of goods, money or information) between organisations and/or individuals. Typical examples of transactions include:

- Purchases or returns by a customer
- Invoices for goods or services
- Payments for goods, services, or against a debt
- Credits – for example, a bank customer pays money into their account
- Debits – a customer withdraws money from their account
- Interest – a bank charges interest on a loan
- Payroll – an organisation pays its employees
- Reservations (cinema tickets, hotel rooms, flights etc.)
- Lending – a library lends books to customers
- Donations to a charity

For each of these transactions, data is recorded. Some of this data is essential for the day-to-day running of the business – a bank, for example, cannot afford to lose a single transaction. Other data, such as exactly what purchases a particular customer makes in a supermarket each time they go shopping, is not quite as essential. If they forget their loyalty card one week, the missing data will not materially affect the company.

But data is the life-blood of many organisations. Knowing what a customer regularly purchases, for example, enables the supermarket to send them relevant advertising and special offers. Knowing what size of donation has been made in the past by a particular donor enables a charity to ask for an appropriate amount in their next targeted mailing, thus maximising their revenue.

Dear Bilal

Thank you for your generous donation last year of **£200**.

Without your support we could not provide the vital services we offer to help others. Please consider a further donation this year which would enable us to continue our work in your community.

Yes, I will help transform lives, families and communities by making a gift today.

Here is my gift of:

☐ £200 ☐ £300 ☐ £500 ☐ My choice of £ _____

Targeted marketing

Targeted marketing identifies an audience that is likely to buy products or services. Once this group has been identified, an organisation can develop a service or product and marketing campaign specifically aimed at these people. For example, a car dealer may wish to advertise their latest electric car model to a group of people who have shown an interest in environmental issues or electric cars and live within twenty miles of the dealership.

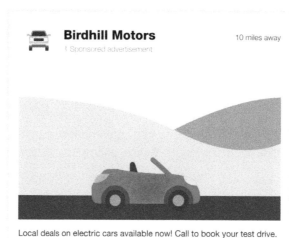

Local deals on electric cars available now! Call to book your test drive.

Marketing campaigns may include online, television and print advertisements. Social media companies such as Facebook and Twitter will advertise to a given number of their followers (depending on the level of payment from the organisation wishing to advertise) who satisfy particular criteria.

Companies can pay Google to place targeted ads on its site. Personalised advertising enables advertisers to reach users based on their interests, demographics, physical location and other criteria.

(*Read more about targeted marketing in the next chapter, under the heading 'Data analysis'.*)

Collaborative working

For employees, collaborative working may be more enjoyable and more satisfying than working in isolation on a project. Shared problem-solving may lead to better solutions, as different team members may have different ideas and skills that they can contribute. Technology makes it possible to work from home, with flexible hours, and still be part of a team.

For an employer, collaborative working may have several benefits. It may mean that new employees, working in a team with more experienced workers, get up to speed more quickly. Things are less likely to go badly wrong if knowledge, information and best practice are shared between employees. If a key employee leaves, someone else should be able to take over their role.

Working in isolation can mean:

- Managers, team leaders and teammates may miss important updates because they can't see them.
- Team members may waste time searching for information, or duplicating work.
- Managers and team leaders don't know what their teams are working on or what stage a project has reached and waste time holding team meetings.

There are many software solutions that enable collaborative working. These can be crucial when people in a team are working in different locations and different time zones.

Collaboration tools can make it easy to:

- share ideas and have group chats to discuss projects
- attach files to a chat using drag and drop to share
- pin important messages to files and access them whenever needed
- stay on top of projects with shared to-do lists and reminders
- get instant feedback on ideas with polls
- integrate with third-party apps such as Google Drive, Google Calendar, Twitter and more

Exercises

1. Elizabeth is a senior citizen who lives in the countryside, nine miles from the nearest town. She has recently purchased a tablet computer and has learned how to use applications including email, Internet browsing software and online shopping. She is planning to start doing her banking online.

    (a) Explain **two** services that she will be able to take advantage of when she starts online banking. [4]

    (b) Describe the impact that using online services may have on Elizabeth. [6]

2. Henry is a software developer who works for AGR Software, a company which specialises in creating company websites. The management is considering investing in software which will enable the seven software designers and developers to work collaboratively.

    (a) Describe **two** features that such software is likely to include. [4]

    (b) Describe the impact and implications of collaborative working for:

    (i) management [4]

    (ii) Henry and the other members of the team. [4]

3. Az owns a small high street store selling scarves, socks, and fashion accessories.
    He contracts AGR Software to design a website for his company, on which he will advertise his stock.
    He plans to start selling online.

    (a) Describe **two** implications for Az of contracting another company to build his website. [4]

    (b) Once the website is successfully up and running, he will be able to collect the name, address and email address of everyone who buys online, as well as the items they bought and their value.

    Describe **two** ways in which he can use the data he collects to build his online sales. [4]

Chapter 26
IT systems in organisations

Objectives

- Describe the features and implications of IT systems used by organisations for: stock control, data logging, data analysis, general office tasks, creative tasks, advertising, manufacturing, security

Stock control systems

Stock control, or inventory control, systems are needed to keep track of how much stock an organisation has at any one time, how fast each item is moving and when it needs to be reordered. It applies to every item needed to produce a product or service, from raw materials to finished goods. Data is input at every stage of the production process, from purchase and delivery to using and re-ordering stock.

Thousands of different organisations need to control their stock; from huge organisations like the NHS, Amazon, supermarkets with hundreds of thousands of different items, to small manufacturing businesses, and restaurants.

A good stock control system will ensure that an organisation holds the right amount of stock in the right place at the right time. Holding too much stock ties up capital unnecessarily. Not holding enough means that sometimes stock will run out. It is necessary to record for each item, how many are used or sold in a day, a week or a month, how many hours or days between ordering and receiving new stock, quantity discounts on stock, supplier details and so on.

 Describe an organisation that holds stock. What are the possible consequences of running out of stock?

A computerised stock control system

Typically, this will include:

- Stock and pricing data integrated with accounting and invoicing systems. Whenever a sale is made, the stock quantity is automatically adjusted in the stock control system. When a purchase order is entered into the accounting system, the stock system will record that stock is "on order". This means that data only has to be entered once into the system.

- Automatic stock monitoring, with an order being automatically produced when an item of stock reaches a pre-defined re-order level.

- Barcoding systems so that the computer system can print and read bar codes.

- Radio Frequency Identification (RFID) which enables individual products or components to be tracked throughout the supply chain.

RFID technology

RFID enables an organisation to identify individual products and components and to track them throughout the supply chain from production to point of sale. The technology uses radio waves to enable communication between a tag and a reading device. (See Chapter 3.)

- Readers can be placed at different positions within a factory or warehouse to show when and where goods are moved.

- The information that the reader collects is processed by the stock control software.

Checking stock in a warehouse using RFID

RFID tag attached to a garment

RFID tagging can also be used for security, by positioning tag-readers at points of high risk, such as exits, and causing them to trigger alarms.

Name and describe some other applications of RFID technology.

Data logging

There are several different types of data logger, used in numerous indoor, outdoor, underwater and temperature-controlled environments. A web-based data logging system, for example, can enable round-the-clock data to be collected in remote locations, and transmitted via a secure web server to a website where it can be accessed and monitored.

Applications of data logging include environmental monitoring, sports training, security monitoring and monitoring of patients' vital signs in hospitals.

Case study: Water level loggers help save sea turtle nests

Florida State University researchers are collaborating with the U.S. Fish and Wildlife Service and conservation groups to identify sea turtle nesting areas at high risk of groundwater inundation. Sea turtle embryos can only develop properly in a narrow range of incubation conditions, and among the most critical is an appropriate level of moisture – not enough and they shrivel and die, too much and they drown.

In the summer of 2017, HOBO® Water Level data Loggers were positioned at 11 loggerhead sea turtle nests. Around 100 eggs are laid in each nest. The purpose is to provide insight into the water inundation tolerance levels of the developing eggs. Volunteers can then monitor nests laid in vulnerable areas and move them closer to the dunes. This can only be done within 12 hours of the nest being laid, however, as moving the nests later than that can cause the embryos to die.

Task: Research another application of data loggers. How are they used in this application? What information do they give? What advantages do they have in the situation you describe? Prepare a presentation on your findings and analysis.

Data analysis

Data may be collected by any one of numerous methods – for example by data logging, observation, stock control systems, store loyalty cards, Internet usage. **Big Data** refers to the huge data sets collected by organisations around the world. Social media companies collect so much data that they can only analyse a small fraction of it. In 2016 it was estimated that only 0.5% of all data collected was ever analysed.

Customer Relationship Management (CRM) systems use analytics to recognise emerging patterns and identify trends. This can help organisations to control how they interact with their customers. Data analysed includes sales figures and data on individual customer purchases. Companies may also use customer surveys to find out their views about the company – enabling them to improve products and services as well as provide more efficient communication and customer service when needed. The goals of a CRM are to help an organisation to:

- increase customer satisfaction
- become more efficient
- produce better marketing campaigns
- attract new customers
- boost sales

CRM systems are used by small companies with turnovers of around £1 million, to the largest companies in the world. They are also used in many other organisations such as the education, health and charities sectors.

Case study: Tesco Clubcard scheme and CRM

Tesco is the third largest retailer in the world, measured by revenue, with stores in 14 countries across Asia, Europe and North America. Their aggressive marketing and CRM strategies have played a central role in helping them to maintain their competitive advantage. They have different loyalty schemes for different family members: Tesco Kids Club, Tesco Baby and Toddler Club, Tesco Healthy Living Club, World of Wine Club.

Data collected via these schemes allows them to carry out targeted marketing on a vast scale.

- There are over four million variations of its quarterly mailing to ensure that discounts and offers are tailored specifically for the customer.

- Insights gained from the analysis of shopping patterns can be actioned into marketing and retail programs which encourage customer satisfaction and loyalty to Tesco.

- Tesco have been able to create a variety of product ranges to suit different target groups, such as:
  - Healthy Living: Over 400 products which are low in fat and sodium
  - Free From: Produced for people who have food allergies or dietary requirements
  - Special Healthy Kids Snacks: A dedicated range of kids' food products that are high in fibre, fruit and vegetables

Task: Research and describe the benefits of a CRM to an organisation such as a university, retailer, charity or health service provider.

General office tasks

Anyone employed in an office today is probably expected to have a working knowledge of common applications such as word-processing, spreadsheets, web browser software and email software. Proficiency in the advanced features of these packages may be highly valued.

An employee may also be expected to use specialised packages such as accounts, booking systems, payroll, stock control or scheduling software.

Creative tasks

Graphic designers working in many different fields will use specialised software. Websites, films, books, magazines, packaging, advertising and corporate reports all require designers. They combine art and technology to communicate ideas through images, fonts, colours and layouts.

Technical drawings for engineering projects, architectural designs, circuit and product designs are examples of the use of **computer-aided design** (**CAD**) software. Vector-based graphics are used to create two- and three-dimensional images. CAD is used extensively in applications such as computer animation and for special effects in movies.

Modelling with CAD systems offers numerous advantages over traditional drawing methods.

- Designs can be altered without erasing and redrawing.
- 'Zoom' features allow the designer to magnify certain elements of a model to examine it more closely.
- Three-dimensional models can be rotated on any axis to view from any angle.
- Cut-away drawings can be produced to reveal the internal shape of a part.

CAD is often used in conjunction with **computer-aided manufacturing** (**CAM**), which uses the geometrical design data to control automated machinery which manufactures the desired part or product.

Computer-aided design

Advertising

Leading global brands are using IT to attract, engage and retain customers in new and innovative ways. Earlier in this chapter, **targeted** marketing was described. Advertising on **social media** (described in Learning Aim C, Chapter 18) is used by thousands of organisations. **Augmented reality** apps are effective for hundreds of organisations, from selling Pepsi at a football match to selling furniture in Ikea. Try searching for 'Pepsi interactive drink bottles'.

Quick Response (QR) codes are often used in a similar way. Clicking on a QR code can direct users to a web page that contains marketing information and interactivity.

Manufacturing

Automated production lines, robotics and CAD-CAM systems are all used directly in manufacturing goods of all kinds. 3-D printing is revolutionising manufacturing in some areas. One-off prototypes and in some cases, final products, which could never have been produced using traditional manufacturing techniques, can now be made in thousands of prototyping and manufacturing applications including making construction models and materials, prosthetics, jewellery and personalised gifts.

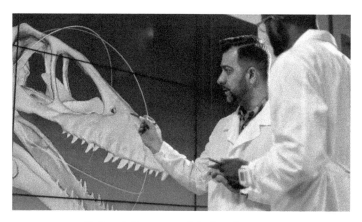

3-D printing a model of a dinosaur

Security

Organisations need security systems to protect them from intruders entering the premises. These could include:

- Alarm systems
- Gates and barriers
- CCTV systems
- Access control to different parts of a building

A typical security system for a small business includes a control panel, door and window sensors, motion sensors (both interior and exterior), wired or wireless security cameras and a high-decibel siren or alarm.

Exercises

1. Some areas in the UK are prone to flooding. John is in charge of ensuring, as far as possible, that people whose homes and businesses are in danger of flooding are given sufficient warning to take whatever measures they can and if necessary evacuate their premises.

   (a) State **four** items of data that will be helpful in assessing an immediate danger of flooding. [4]

   (b) Explain **three** ways in which information technology can be used to help John to decide when a flood warning should be issued. [6]

2. Ana is in charge of the stock control system at Anderson Building Supplies, a builder's merchant selling tools and materials. The sales and accounting system automatically updates stock levels whenever stock is sold, purchased, returned or written off as damaged.

   RFID technology is used in the stock control system to record the stock levels of each stock item in a warehouse when a manual stock count is performed every six months.

   (a) Explain **two** reasons why it is necessary to do a manual stock count. [4]

   (b) Describe how RFID technology works. [4]

   (c) A unique stock ID and a description of each different stock item are held in the stock control system.

   State **four** other data items that are held in the stock control system to help ensure that no item unexpectedly becomes out of stock. [4]

   (d) Explain **three** ways in which RFID technology may be used to reduce theft and shoplifting incidents. [4]

Chapter 27
Impact of IT systems on organisations

Objectives

- Describe the impact and implications for organisations of IT systems in terms of:
  - user experience – ease of use, performance, availability, accessibility
  - employee and customer needs
  - cost
  - implementation – timescales, testing, downtime
  - replacement or integration with current systems
  - productivity
  - working practices
  - staff training needs (initial and ongoing)
  - user support
  - security

The user experience

The success of an IT system may depend to a large extent on factors such as:

- **Ease of use** – How easy it is to use and the fluidity and familiarity of the interface.

- **Performance** – How long it takes to perform a typical task.

- **Availability** – Whether the software is always available or if technical problems frequently affect its downtime.

- **Accessibility** – How many people can access the system regardless of their device type, abilities or disabilities.

All organisations interact with customers. If they have an online presence, they must make sure their customers or clients find the organisation's website easy to use and a generally pleasant experience. The website must cater for experienced users as well as users who are only just getting to grips with purchasing goods, banking, booking a taxi or holiday or any of hundreds of other online tasks.

Ease of use

Online data entry must be:

- **as simple as possible**, with clear and consistent navigation

- **predictable** – users should not be wondering "What happens if I press this button?"

- **forgiving** – users must be able to backtrack easily if they make a mistake

- **consistent with what users expect** – for example the term 'shopping cart' is familiar to almost all online shoppers, so it would be counter-intuitive to use a different term

A large supermarket has recently been experiencing problems with some items in customers' online orders. It regularly happens that customers order, for example, '5kg of bananas' when they intend to order 5 bananas.
Suggest how this type of error could be avoided.

Performance

The overall performance of a system will have an effect on the productivity of a workforce. A system which responds immediately to user requests and makes routine tasks quicker and easier for the user will ensure that tasks can be completed in a faster time and lead to a more productive workforce.

Availability

Broadband services may sometimes be disrupted or unavailable, leaving millions of customers unable to connect to websites. Organisations using cloud software are particularly vulnerable, since they will not be able to use essential software until the problem is fixed.

A website must respond quickly to user requests. "Please wait" messages can cause customers to switch immediately to an alternative site. If an organisation's computer system is not available for any reason, this can have serious consequences for users.

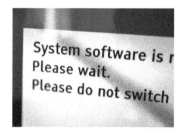

Case study: Visa card meltdown

In 2018, 5.2 million card transactions failed across Europe in a 24-hour period when a hardware problem caused a system failure. Queues built up at petrol stations, shopping was left at supermarket tills and people were unable to pay for meals they had already eaten at restaurants. Thousands of merchants had to close and sustained heavy financial losses.

Accessibility

A computer system should be made accessible to as many employees and customers as possible, through appropriate design of both hardware and software. Hardware devices include:

- Microphone to enable verbal input
- Speakers/headphones for audio output
- Concept keyboard to enable a disabled person to input text
- Braille display to convert screen output to Braille
- Large monitor with large text for a partially sighted person
- Specially adapted mouse or trackball

Special keyboard for blind or partially-sighted users

Operating system software may provide:

- Adjustable screen resolution, brightness, text size, contrast etc., to suit individual users
- Audio description of screen elements such as images or menus, audio instructions for navigation
- Enlarged on-screen keyboard to facilitate data entry

Employee and customer needs

The next few paragraphs describe some of the impact and implications of introducing a new IT system. Different systems (a new website, stock control, manufacturing systems, etc.,) will have many similar issues as well as impacts and implications specific to different departments.

Case study: A garden centre

Imagine you are the commercial director in a small firm selling seeds, plants, shrubs and trees to individuals and organisations.

A new IT system is to be implemented. Before deciding on a new system, a lot of research and planning needs to take place.

- What is the main goal of the new system? Is it to improve your relationship with customers? Organise all your contacts in one place? Enhance your marketing campaigns?
- What do employees expect from a new system? You must evaluate their wants and needs.
- Impact on employees. Will it improve efficiency? Will it be easy and intuitive to use? Is the transition to the new system likely to go smoothly?
- Will customers benefit from the new system? What form will the benefits take – cheaper products, advice on planting, special offers, invitations to special events?

Cost

A cost-benefit analysis needs to be carried out to estimate the likely long-term benefits of any new system. Will they outweigh the short-term costs? Costs can include:

- Paying interest on a loan to cover the initial capital cost
- system maintenance costs
- staff training costs

Implementation

A plan of action to include a strict timeline should be made well in advance of implementation. Every aspect needs to be thoroughly tested and training sessions scheduled, preferably in the least busy sales season. Backup copies of all data should be made to ensure that no important information is lost during the transition.

If the new system is an online system involving customers, this will need to be taken into account. Implementation may involve some downtime, and if this is scheduled for the least busy period of the year, it will affect the fewest customers. A prominent notice on the company's website explaining the necessity for this, and the likely benefits to customers, will mitigate the inconvenience they may experience.

Replacement or integration with current systems

Replacing an existing system can be an expensive and time-consuming business. A company may decide that it is outgrowing its current financial systems, and it needs a new system which provides better or more detailed information, is easier to use, or provides better performance for a growing volume of sales.

However, it may not be easy to migrate all the existing data from the old system to the new system. Transfer of data may be complex and require specialist help from the company providing the new system. Historical data such as which customers have purchased which items, or sales figures for different periods in the past, may no longer be available on the new system.

It may be necessary to run the old and the new system in parallel for a period of time to ensure that it works correctly, and that staff operate it correctly. This will mean extra work for the staff.

Implementation of a new system should be done, for example, in a quiet sales period of the year, when downtime and any disruption to normal routines will be minimised.

Staff training needs

Before a new system goes live, it is essential to allow enough time for employees to learn and understand the software. They need to have one-to-one sessions with someone who thoroughly understands the software, so that they can ask questions and have demonstrations of how it will work. When the system is up and running and the basic uses of the software mastered, it is likely that more training will be required as more advanced features are revealed.

One-to-one training sessions are useful for training users

Productivity

Many IT systems are designed to increase productivity. For example:

- Cloud-based systems allow collaborative working.
- Stock control systems integrated with the sales order processing system can speed up routine tasks. This can eliminate the need to hire extra staff.
- General office or creative tasks can be performed better and more efficiently with appropriate software.

Working practices

Staff may have to work in a different way after the introduction of a new system. Ask for feedback from the affected employees and make sure they are comfortable with the new software. Is the user interface easy and intuitive? Are there improvements that could be made? Does the system provide all the information they need?

In many organisations, employees may be able to work from home for some or all of the week. They may need access to software and data held in the cloud or on the office server. Their hours of work may be flexible, but this does not necessarily mean that they are available 24 hours a day. Working conditions need to be established.

User support

Most organisations will either have their own IT department to provide technical support to users or alternatively, have a contract with a specialist firm to provide support. This may involve considerable ongoing expense, but without it, even simple user problems may result in frustration, loss of productivity and missed deadlines. Technical support can be carried out using remote desktop technology, so that a technician is able to see the user's screen and operate their computer remotely to fix a problem.

Security

External security precautions were discussed in the last chapter. Internal security systems to protect data and systems include anti-virus software and firewalls. All users must be trained in keeping data secure on mobile devices used outside company premises, proper use of passwords and other techniques for protecting data and systems. These issues were discussed in Learning Aim D.

Exercises

1. Donald has recently set up a small company called Fresh'n'Tasty which sells weekly vegetable boxes containing seasonal vegetables and fruit, mostly grown by local farmers, to subscription customers.

   Some customers have complained, especially in winter months, that they do not like the selection of vegetables such as carrots, turnips and cabbage, and they have cancelled their subscriptions.

   Donald wants to give his customers a choice of available vegetables and fruit each week. He is in the process of having a new website designed to enable this.

   (a) Describe **three** factors he should take into account when designing the user interface on his website. [6]
   (b) Describe **two** possible impacts on employees, filling and delivering the vegetable boxes for each customer, of the new system. [4]

2. Ted owns a small company which makes garden furniture. He has a simple computerised accounts system, but the business is expanding and it no longer fulfils all his requirements.

   Ted decides that he must switch to a new system which will make it easier for sales staff to process sales, and also provide more management information.

   (a) Describe **two** factors that will impact the sales staff who work with the new system. [4]
   (b) Discuss the impact that installing a new system may have on the business. [8]

Chapter 28
Sourcing and collecting data

Objectives

Describe:

- sources of data:
  - Primary
  - Secondary
- methods of judging and ensuring the reliability of data

- the characteristics and implications of methods of collecting data and opinions:
  - survey
  - questionnaire
  - focus groups
  - interview
- the characteristics and implications of user interfaces for data collection and processing systems: ease of use, accessibility, error reduction, intuitiveness, functionality, performance, compatibility

Primary data

Data which is collected for a specific purpose is called primary data. Methods of collecting the data will vary according to the type of information being collected and the goals of the research. In this chapter we will assume that information is being collected by an organisation in order to:

- provide a better service or a more useful product

- increase its customer base or customer satisfaction

- better understand the needs and concerns of its employees

Survey

Surveys are a good way of collecting a large amount of data from a given population. A population may be all the inhabitants of a country, a town, a school, all the existing or potential customers or clients of a particular business or organisation, or some other chosen group of people. A survey should be designed to give an adequate answer to at least one specific question, and it requires careful preparation. It may well be that the survey will lead to other, unexpected insights as well.

A survey involves asking questions of respondents, and may be carried out in person, by phone or online. It typically collects three types of information:

Type	Description	Example
Description	Information about respondents	Age, income, location
Behaviour	Information about respondents' behaviours	Existing customer? Typical amount spent?
Preferences	Respondents' opinions	Preference for certain products, opinion about service/product

Most people prefer short multiple-choice questions. Response rates to surveys are generally low – they can be improved by offering participants some incentive to participate, such as a gift or the chance of winning something in a lottery.

Questionnaire

A questionnaire is similar to a survey but is likely to be sent to existing clients or customers who have recently made a purchase, used a particular product or service, or work for the organisation using the questionnaire.

This is a typical first screen in an online questionnaire. Notice that all screens have the option to go back to the previous screen:

Questionnaires for existing customers often ask how far you agree with a statement:

Quantitative and qualitative data

Questions of the form "on a scale of 1-5, how far do you agree with the following statement" are commonly used in gathering opinions. This type of data is called **quantitative** data. Answers in the form of a numerical value are much easier to analyse; for example, spreadsheet formulas can be used to do quite detailed analyses of answers.

However, sometimes a survey may ask the respondent to give a reason for their answer:

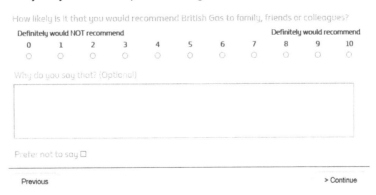

Analysis becomes much more complex with this type of **qualitative** data. The first step for the researcher is to understand clearly:

- What are we trying to understand?
- What could we change about the product or service based on the hypothetical findings?

A researcher may be asked to look for common reasons for dissatisfaction, thus helping the organisation to understand how their product or service could be improved. They may also want to pick up on trends and discover opportunities.

Q1 The questionnaire above asks the user to give a reason for their answer. How will this be analysed? Why does British Gas ask this question?

Q2 Suppose that an existing customer has logged in to the British Gas website. They complete a questionnaire regarding their experience with the website. What action could British Gas take if the customer answers "No" to the question below?

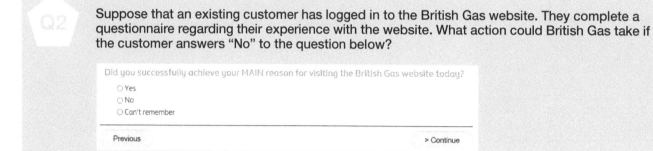

Did you successfully achieve your MAIN reason for visiting the British Gas website today?

○ Yes
○ No
○ Can't remember

Previous   > Continue

Focus groups

Focus groups are groups of people invited to come together to discuss a particular issue, planned strategy or product. Typically a focus group includes between eight and 12 participants, and a moderator to guide the discussion.

Selecting people for a focus group

- Define the purpose of the group: identify the goal of the discussion. For example, if the goal of the focus group is to test a new product, you will want to identify participants who have used similar products or are interested in similar products.

- Screen the participants: Choose members that are either past, current or prospective users of the product or service under investigation. Customer lists are a good source, and advertising on social media is another way to recruit participants. It may be necessary to offer an incentive to participate.

The people making up the focus group need to be selected with care so that they are a realistic representation of the likely customer base. It may be necessary to hold several meetings with different focus groups in different locations.

Using open-ended questions

Open-ended questions are widely used in focus groups since the aim is to gather ideas and opinions by carrying out qualitative rather than quantitative research. Examples of open-ended questions are:

"What do you like best about Product A?"
"How could Product B be improved?"

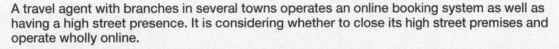

A travel agent with branches in several towns operates an online booking system as well as having a high street presence. It is considering whether to close its high street premises and operate wholly online.

(a) Suggest how it may recruit people for a focus group to gauge the attitude of potential customers to this proposal.

(b) Suggest some questions that should be asked in the focus group.

(c) Suggest how the information gathered in the focus group would be analysed.

Interview

Interviews are time-consuming and generally used infrequently as a method of gathering information which can be analysed digitally. Job interviews are the most common example, and usually reveal far more about a candidate for a job than could be gathered by any other means.

When a new IT system is to be introduced, interviews will be conducted with several people from top management to selected employees who will be involved with the system. This is the best way for both the systems analyst and the organisation to ensure that requirements are thoroughly understood and that there are no misunderstandings. The interviewer must have questions ready in advance, but must also be prepared to respond to answers and possibly take a different line of questioning.

A major problem with this method of collecting data and opinions, for both parties, is finding time for lengthy interviews.

Secondary data

Secondary data is quantitative data that has already been collected by someone other than the user. It requires much less time to collect since the data is very likely already held in a database and accessible via government records and various online and offline resources.

Secondary data has typically been collected by researchers who have had years of experience in recruiting representative sample populations, designing surveys and questionnaires, and using specific measurement tools. On the negative side, it may not provide data in the format you need – for example, it could refer to a different geographical region, or ask respondents to specify an age range when you need an actual age.

Judging and ensuring the reliability of data

A weakness of both primary and secondary data is that you cannot always rely on the accuracy of the data. The researcher will need to establish and critically evaluate how the data was gathered and presented. In addition, the data may be out-of-date in rapidly changing circumstances.

Characteristics and implications of user interfaces for data collection and processing systems

The **user interface** determines how users interact with an online survey or registration form.

Ease of use

If someone filling in a survey finds it difficult to enter data quickly and accurately, or there are too many questions to answer, they may give up and not bother to complete the survey. If they make a mistake and are unable to correct it without starting all over again, they will give up.

- It is much quicker and easier for a user to click in a box, or select from a drop-down list of options, than to type in text.

- Having just one question per screen makes the interface easier to use.

- Two well-placed buttons labelled **Next** and **Previous** may be all that are needed in the way of navigation.

Accessibility

The interface should be made accessible to people with a disability. For example, a partially-sighted person may need to be able to change the size of text without the text scrolling off the screen. Colours should be chosen carefully and take into consideration those with colour blindness. Voice recognition and input may be used.

Error reduction

Input errors on data collection forms can be reduced by minimizing the amount of data that is input. Multiple choice questions, where the user simply has to click one button, are commonly used.

Data validation is another way of ensuring that answers are reasonable. Range checks for numeric fields, length checks, character checks and type checks may be made on fields of different types. Validation checks are described in more detail in the next chapter.

Verification of input can take different forms. If, for example, a product code or error code is entered, the screen can display the description of the product or error to give visual confirmation that the code was correctly input.

Intuitiveness

The interface should be designed in such a way that users will find it **intuitive**. What a user finds intuitive, however, may depend on their level of knowledge and experience of similar interfaces.

Using standard icons and navigation methods is one step in the design of an intuitive user interface. However, if you have ever changed from an iPhone to an Android, or watched a toddler swiping the TV screen to get to the next page, you will know that this does not always guarantee results.

Functionality

User interface design focuses on anticipating what users might want to do. Interface elements include:

- input controls: buttons, text fields, checkboxes, radio buttons, dropdown lists, list boxes, toggles, date field

- navigational components: menus, search fields, icons, sliders

- informational components: tooltips, icons, progress bar, notifications, message boxes

Sometimes a designer may intentionally make functionality as easy as possible for some tasks, and difficult for other tasks.

Case study: Amazon interface

Amazon makes the process of returning a purchased item fairly straightforward. Once the customer has found the right button on the order form, they are guided through the process of printing a shipping label and returning the product.

Amazon aims to guide you towards their online system for Customer Services though there is a phone number to call Amazon's customer service centre. Since handling calls from customers is expensive and time consuming, the company encourage online and email communication which is far more cost effective, though it may be inconvenient for some customers.

Performance and compatibility

The day after "Black Friday" in November 2018 (a day when shops discount their products to attract shoppers in the run-up to Christmas), Argos reported that half of its orders had been made from a handset, up from 40% the previous year. As more and more people use mobile devices to do their shopping and banking, organisations need to ensure that their websites are compatible with these devices, and that a high-level performance is maintained on all devices.

Exercises

1. Complete the following table showing the differences between research using primary and secondary data.

	Primary data	Secondary data
Definition	Factual, first-hand data collected by the user	
Type of data	Real-time data	
Conducted by		Another person or organisation
Needs		May not directly address the researcher's needs
Involvement	Researcher is very involved	
Time taken to collect data		
Cost		Low

2. Jodi owns an Art Gallery. She is investigating the possibility of holding an Art Fair in a suitable location in London to sell contemporary art. She intends this to become an annual event.

   Jodi needs to do some preliminary research to help her judge whether the proposed venture will be a financial success.

   (a) (i) Describe **two** methods she could use to gather primary data. [4]

       (ii) State **one** advantage of each of these methods. [2]

   (b) Describe **one** advantage and **one** disadvantage of using secondary data rather than primary data to help Jodi make a decision. [4]

   (c) Describe **two** characteristics of the interface that will speed up data entry. [4]

3. Nathan is a member of the sales team at a company selling classroom furniture to primary schools. He uses a sales and accounting package to enter order details from schools placing orders online, by telephone or mail in order to create an invoice. Most of the contact details and addresses for UK primary schools are already held in the system.

   (a) Describe **two** methods that the software can use to help ensure accuracy of data entered. [4]

   (b) Describe **two** characteristics of the interface that will speed up data entry. [4]

Chapter 29
Using and manipulating data

Objectives

- Describe the uses, processes and implications for individuals and organisations of accessing and using data and information in digital form

- Explain reasons for ensuring data accuracy

- Describe methods of ensuring accuracy: verification and validation

- Describe methods of extracting and sorting data

- Describe numerical and data modelling

- Describe the presentation of data and results

Uses of data

In the last chapter various methods of collecting data were described. Data and information are collected for different reasons.

The data collected by means of **surveys** and **questionnaires** may be used to ascertain the level of customer satisfaction with the organisation's products or services. This data, once analysed, may be used to pinpoint changes or improvements that need to be made in order to maintain or increase sales.

Data collected from **focus groups** is often used when planning a new product, to canvas opinions on the likely success and level of demand. It can be used to test different packaging or names for a product, to find out which is the most popular.

Interviews (excluding interviews for prospective employees) are conducted when there are certain key people who are able to impart information about the needs of a department or company which can only be discovered by in-depth questioning. This is crucially important for, say, a systems analyst who is creating a new information technology system for a company.

Data accuracy

Data is also collected through the day-to-day operations of an organisation. Every time a sale, purchase, payment or receipt is recorded, data is entered into the IT system, some of it manually, some of it using an input device such as a barcode reader, magnetic stripe reader, RFID or some other method.

Ideally, as little data as possible should be input manually. Some data may have to be input by customers or clients, and some by employees using the IT system.

Julie visits a travel agent in October and books a holiday, including flight and hotel, for her family. They are planning to spend Christmas with another family on a Greek island and she books for one week leaving on 20th December.

Unfortunately, the travel agent makes a data entry error and books them in for 2nd December. The error is not discovered until late November.

What are the consequences for the family, and for the travel agent, of this error? How could it have been avoided?

Verification and validation

When data is entered manually, every attempt must be made to ensure that it is entered accurately. Data may be **verified** by being asked to type it in twice (common for setting a password), or by displaying options and allowing the user to select the correct one.

- Entering an address typically involves entering the postcode, and then selecting the correct address from a few options stored on the computer system.

- When a product code is entered, the product description may be displayed on the screen.

Validation means using an algorithm to ensure that the data entered is reasonable. Validation usually cannot ensure complete accuracy; a date of birth, for example, can conform to validation rules and still not be correct.

Validation checks include:

- Type check – entry should be all alphabetic or all numeric characters, for example
- Range check – if 153 is entered for a person's age, this will be rejected
- Format check – a valid postcode must conform to one of a set of possible formats
- Length check – an employee number might have to be exactly 6 numeric digits
- Presence check – data has to be entered in a particular field

Form controls such as list boxes, group boxes, buttons, check boxes, option buttons, combo boxes, scroll bars and spin buttons all make it easier for users to enter data accurately.

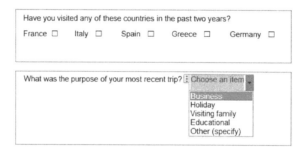

Check box and combo box controls

The screenshot below shows a database form used to enter data about pupils entering a competition. The user cannot enter a figure for Age which is outside the range 11-17.

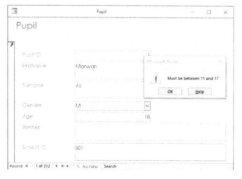

Validating an input field

 What other validation checks could be performed on the data input using the above form?

Extracting and sorting data

Once data has been collected, using for example a survey or questionnaire, it needs to be analysed in order to extract useful information. This may be done in different ways, for example:

- using a spreadsheet or a database
- using a special-purpose software package for analysing data and producing results

Using such software, data can be sorted into different categories, filtered in different ways and totalled. Reports and graphs can be produced showing the results in different ways. Database queries may be used to extract data matching given criteria, for example:

```
(dateOfManufacture > #01/01/2016#) AND (productionCost > 5000)
```

Surveys on consumers' shopping habits are frequently done. The bar chart below shows results of a typical survey of consumers aged between 18 and 70.

Suppose data on shopping habits has been collected by an organisation which specialises in carrying out surveys.

Describe how the data could be collected to ensure that it gives an accurate picture of the general population's shopping habits.

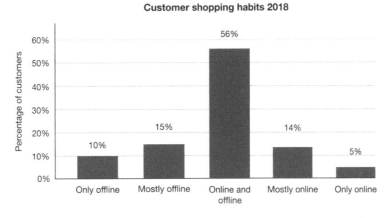

Results of a survey carried out by an independent organisation

Look at the data in the survey above.

(a) Is there anything about this data analysis that you find surprising?

(b) Which age groups do you think fall into the "Only Offline" and "Only online" categories?

(c) How could this information be useful to a retailer?

Numerical and data modelling

Numerical modelling is frequently used in civil engineering, on projects such as road or railway bridges to calculate, for example, the effects on the structure of moving loads.

Modelling techniques are also used to predict the consequences of certain trends, activities or planned actions. Climate change models, for example, use temperature, level of greenhouse gas emissions and other data collected over many years to predict how the earth's temperature will probably rise over the next 20, 50 or 100 years, and the likely consequences of such a rise.

An individual or organisation planning a new enterprise may construct a numerical model to inform a decision on whether the enterprise is likely to be successful. If, for example, an individual is planning to open a market stall selling bread, they may input data such as:

- Cost of ingredients, electricity, labour etc.
- Cost of renting market stall
- Average number of people visiting market every Saturday
- Estimated sales volume
- Prices charged

The model will then calculate the profit. Each of the input data values can be changed to perform "What if" calculations to see the effect on profit:

"What if I increase the prices by 10%, and decrease the sales volume by 20%?"

Presenting the results of a numerical model

The output from a numerical model may be presented in the form of a tabulated report, an infographic, linear graph or bar chart. The model may be interactive, allowing the user to enter various parameters and obtain instant answers to their questions.

The accuracy of the model can be determined by comparing its predictions with actual results, after the enterprise has been going for a certain amount of time. If the model predicts outcomes fairly accurately, it can be rolled out when new projects are planned. If it is not accurate, adjustments can be made in retrospect to see what parameters give the best results before using the model again.

Exercises

1. Val works for a small company that manufactures three types of vacuum cleaner: industrial, home use and hand-held.

    (a) She has been asked to prepare a presentation showing:

    - The annual turnover for each of these products during the past year
    - The monthly sales value for each product

    Explain, with reasons, a suitable format for the type of chart that should be used for presentation of these figures. [4]

    (b) Val has also been asked to analyse the results of 320 surveys completed online by customers who have bought products. The data from the survey is held in a spreadsheet, containing for each completed questionnaire:

    - The name and email address of the person who completed the survey
    - Their answers to six questions indicating, in a range of 1 (very dissatisfied) to 5 (completely satisfied), their satisfaction with features of the product and the service they received from the company.
    - Boxes asking customers to explain the reason for their score to each question are included.

    Val's analysis shows an average satisfaction value of 4.2 for the quality of the product, but only 2.6 for the quality of the service they received from the company.

    Describe **three** implications for management and employees of these results. [6]

2. Anthony works for a charity which supplies surplus food from the food industry which would otherwise be wasted, to frontline charities. These include hostels for homeless people, children's breakfast clubs, lunch clubs for older people, domestic violence refuges and community cafés.

    Anthony is in charge of the system which manages the receipt of food, inventory and stock rotation and allocation of food to member charities. The data from each transaction is held in a database on the system.

    (a) Describe **three** validation checks that could be carried out on data being entered. [6]

    (b) Describe **two** other techniques which can be used on an input form to help the user enter data accurately. [4]

    (c) Explain **two** ways in which the data collected may be used. [4]

LEARNING AIM F

Issues

In this section:

Chapter 30
Privacy and ethical behaviour

Objectives

- Describe the moral and ethical factors relating to the use of information technology:
  - online behaviour and netiquette
  - privacy
  - freedom of speech and censorship
  - acceptable use

Online behaviour and netiquette

"Etiquette" is a framework of rules and customs governing how people behave, and what constitutes good manners. **Netiquette** refers to the rules and customs which provide guidelines for good manners on the Internet. This might include, for example, being polite, respectful, friendly, honest and straightforward in emails that you send to different people.

Email etiquette

In the same way that there are rules and customs for laying out a business or personal letter, there are some guidelines that you should follow when writing an email.

When writing a business email:

- Always include a subject line.

- Use the recipient's name in the greeting line or start with Dear Sir or Madam.

- Don't use texting abbreviations in business emails or write in uppercase letters.

- Read through your email and make sure its contents are clear, appropriate, necessary and correctly spelt.

- Choose an appropriate close such as Yours faithfully, *Regards*, *Thanks* or *Best wishes*.

- Take care what you write – your email may remain on the company server forever and could be used as evidence against you in a future dispute.

F

Online behaviour

Social media sites such as Facebook, Twitter, YouTube and others have little control over the posts made and watched by their billions of users. The vast majority of users use social media to keep in touch with friends, share photographs, read about the latest news and current affairs, seek information about products, and so on.

However, some posts contain hate speech, videos with violent or traumatising content, or content that is harmful to children.

Online gaming can lead to addiction. An 18-year-old girl reported, "It was sad that I didn't notice how soon I replaced the people I actually knew in life for others online. I never noticed the time of night and somehow felt this urge so that I couldn't stop playing."

Privacy on the Internet

Hundreds of different organisations hold data about each of us without our being aware of it. Your **digital footprint** is the information that is stored about you as you visit websites, send email and use social media networks. If you have location tracking activated on your mobile phone, you can see a timeline of where you have been from the first day you started using Google on your phone. Google also knows every site you have ever visited from each device you use. Using this data, it can create an advertisement profile based on your information, including your location, gender, age, hobbies, career, interests, products you've bought, photos you've taken, relationship status, income and other attributes.

There is an option for you to download all this data, but it could amount to several gigabytes worth of data so you probably won't want to. Facebook has a similar option to download all your information, including all the contacts in your phone and all the messages, files and audio messages you've ever sent or received.

Your data is stored in a server farm somewhere...

Implications for wider society

In 2018, Facebook was fined £500,000 by the UK's Data Protection watchdog (the maximum fine at the time) for sharing personal information without consent with Cambridge Analytica. This company used information on Facebook users' profiles, likes and dislikes to send micro-targeted ads to millions of users, thus influencing both the UK Brexit vote and the US Presidential election in 2016.

One source suggests that as many as 50,000 variations of adverts were being served every single day on Facebook. Micro-targeted advertising allows a campaign to say completely different, possibly conflicting things to different groups of people.

Case study: Democracy eroded

Many well-informed people hold the opinion that acts by social media companies are destroying democracy.

A former Facebook executive said in 2017 that he feels "tremendous guilt" over his work on "tools that are ripping apart the social fabric of how society works".

Chamath Palihapitiya, who was vice-president for user growth at Facebook before he left the company in 2011, said that he feels tremendous guilt over his work on tools that are ripping apart the social fabric of how society works.

"The short-term, dopamine-driven feedback loops that we have created are destroying how society works. No civil discourse, no cooperation, misinformation, mistruth."

"This is not about Russian ads" he added. *"This is a global problem. It is eroding the core foundations of how people behave by and between each other… you don't realize it, but you are being programmed."*

 Explain briefly how micro-targeting by social media companies works.

Freedom of speech and censorship

Freedom of speech is recognised as a fundamental human right. The Human Rights Act guarantees under the law the rights to freedom of speech and expression. However, this right must be used responsibly and there are exceptions. For example, making comments that are specifically designed to incite racial hatred can be deemed to be a hate crime, and is illegal.

Censorship

Internet censorship in the UK is carried out under a variety of laws, regulations and voluntary arrangements. These include:

- regulations regarding indecent images of children
- English defamation law
- regulations against incitement to terrorism
- copyright law

ISPs sometimes block access to sites that have content relating to drugs, gambling, suicide and self-harm, cyberbullying, criminal skills, hacking and hate.

Cyberbullying is both immoral and unethical

Case study: Sir Tim Berners-Lee on a mission to save the Internet

In November 2018 Sir Tim Berners-Lee, inventor of the World Wide Web, launched a global campaign to save the web from the destructive effects of abuse and discrimination, political manipulation, and other threats that plague the online world.

Berners-Lee said that when the Web started, there was a feeling that it would lead to a world with less conflict, more understanding, better science and good democracy. Instead, we have online abuse, prejudice, bias, polarisation and fake news.

He called on governments, companies and individuals to back a new 'Contract for the Web' that aims to protect people's rights and freedoms on the Internet. The contract will be published in May 2019, by which time half the world's population will be able to get online. More than 50 organisations, including Facebook, have already signed the contract.

Google has also signed up, but Berners-Lee notes that it is developing a censored version of its search engine for the Chinese market. "If you sign up to the principles, you can't do censorship," he said. "Will this be enough to make search engines push back? Will it be persuasive enough for the Chinese government to be more open? I can't predict whether that will happen," he said. Google did not respond for comment.

Acceptable use

Organisations often have their own Acceptable Use Policies, which cover the use and security of their IT systems.

The purpose of such a policy is to establish the acceptable and unacceptable use of electronic devices and network resources in an organisation. It is designed to encourage a culture of ethical and lawful behaviour, openness, trust, and integrity.

It may cover topics such as:

- the creation or downloading of offensive or indecent images, material that is threatening or which promotes discrimination

- attempts to gain unauthorised access to restricted area of the system or to introduce malware

- obligations of the individual to keep passwords secure

 List some of the areas typically covered by a school or college Acceptable Use policy.

Exercises

1. In the first half of 2018, six million accounts were deleted from Twitter. Most of these were bots created to mimic real people, used to spread misinformation, prejudice and biased opinions.

    (a) Explain **two** implications for individuals of receiving multiple micro-targeted messages. [4]

    (b) Describe **two** potential consequences for social media organisations of failing to effectively moderate content on their sites. [4]

2. Mile End College has an Acceptable Use policy regarding the use of technology.

    (a) Explain the purpose of such a policy. [2]

    (b) Describe **two** clauses that may be included in the policy. [4]

Chapter 31
Global and environmental issues

Objectives

- Describe the moral and ethical factors relating to the use of information technology:
  - globalisation
  - unequal access to information technology
  - environmental effects

Globalisation

Globalisation implies interaction between the people, organisations and governments of different nations. Nothing in history has had a greater impact on communication and collaboration across the globe than the invention of the Internet in the early 1980s and the World Wide Web in 1989.

Advances in communication technology, the concepts of cloud storage and cloud computing, and the use of IT in almost every profession and sphere of life, has enabled the exchange of skills and information between people and organisations regardless of geographic location.

Email, social media sites, Skype and other Internet-based communication systems have made it easy and inexpensive to communicate and collaborate with others across the globe.

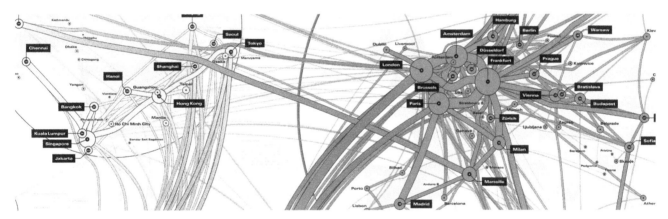

Global communication via the Internet

What are the downsides of the ease of global communication in terms of security and privacy?

Winners and losers in globalisation

Improved technology makes it easy to communicate and share information. Large, global organisations including IBM, Shell, banks and insurance companies have call centres located in countries such as the Philippines or India. Around 600,000 Filipinos are employed in outsourcing, generating billions of dollars for their country's economy.

More specialised and lucrative outsourcing opportunities exist in accounting, animation and gaming, and many of these are outsourced to India and other countries.

F

Large corporations can take advantage of lower tax rates in some countries. Global Internet companies often pay no tax at all in countries where they do huge amounts of business.

- Google, for example, made $7.8bn in revenues in the UK in 2016 out of a global total of $90bn.
- Amazon made $11.3bn in UK revenues in 2017, out of a total of $178bn globally.
- Other tech giants do billions-worth of trade in the UK, but pay little or no tax.

In November 2018, the UK announced that from 2020 it would impose a 2% tax on the UK-generated revenue of these companies.

Problems of globalisation

Some countries do not benefit from globalisation. Infrastructure such as electricity supplies and broadband connections may be patchy or inadequate. In Uganda, for example, only 22% of the country had access to electricity in 2017.

Computer Science and IT lessons in schools are hampered by an electricity supply that may be intermittent, supplied through a single outlet in a classroom, and no broadband connection. UK volunteers who go to developing countries in order to try to close the technology gap often find there are many unexpected difficulties to overcome.

UK volunteers introducing IT to a school in Malawi through the charity RIPPLE Africa

 How can you teach or learn practical computing in a room with no electricity supply? Does the West have a moral obligation to help developing nations catch up?

Unequal access to IT

The so-called **digital divide** exists not only between countries, but also within the UK.

- By June 2018, 95% of homes and offices could get broadband speeds of 24Mbps or faster.
- However, around 1.1 million homes and offices (4% of properties) could not get a fast broadband connection of at least 10Mbps.
- Around 17% of rural premises, and 2% in urban areas, cannot get the broadband speeds necessary to meet their typical needs.

Implications for individuals, organisations and wider society

In the developed parts of the globe, we live in a world dominated by technology. Individuals who have not learned how to use it effectively will get left behind, with fewer opportunities open to them for well-paid, interesting jobs. Those who are not aware of the drawbacks and dangers of some aspects of technology leave themselves exposed to fraud, theft, bullying and lies perpetrated on social media.

Small, rural businesses who do not have access to fast broadband are unable to use technology such as cloud computing, because uploading and downloading data is too slow. They cannot remain competitive in such an environment.

Nations who do not have the infrastructure to support technology will inevitably fall further and further behind the developed nations. Their citizens will be less well-educated and less able to start thriving businesses, the vast majority of which require the use of reliable computers, software and communications.

Environmental issues

Billions of IT devices are used every day around the world. The manufacture of these devices uses enormous quantities of raw materials, precious metals, water and energy.

- Raw materials, including rare earth minerals such as **copper**, **gold**, **lithium** and **platinum** need to be sourced.
- Mines, where these are extracted, can expose workers to toxic substances and dangerous working conditions for low pay.
- Mining may poison soil and groundwater supplies.
- Rainforests in places such as Guyana, Brazil and the Amazon basin are being destroyed.

As well as all the raw materials used in manufacture, there is also a need for:

- materials for packaging
- electricity and gas to power the factories
- diesel and petrol for transportation of raw materials and parts

The use of all these leads to the emission of greenhouse gases and increases our carbon footprint. (A carbon footprint measures the total greenhouse gas emissions caused directly and indirectly by a person, organisation, event or product.)

Huge amounts of water are also used in the manufacture of computers and in the cooling of massive data centres.

Gold mining in Guyana

> **Q3** What are the ethical issues involved here? Is the Western world partially responsible for the destruction of the Amazon rainforest?

Positive environmental issues

In a world in which the population is increasing year on year, technology offers us hope for the future. In thousands of ways, computers have helped us to be more productive and less wasteful. For example, smart, autonomous tractors can plough huge fields entirely guided by GPS, with no wastage of crops when planting or harvesting.

Planting potatoes in Idaho

The ability to work from home means that thousands of workers no longer need to commute to work every day, and so avoid contributing to atmospheric pollution on those journeys.

> **Q4** List some more ways in which technology is helping to solve world problems, rather than contributing to them.

Disposal of devices

Computing devices do not last for more than a few years, and then they have to be disposed of. The milestone of five billion unique mobile subscribers globally was achieved in 2017. Even if every mobile lasts for five years, that's still one billion devices on the scrapheap every year. How long can this trend continue?

The Waste Electrical and Electronics Equipment regulations 2018 (WEEE)

The WEEE Directive, updated in August 2018, requires producers of electrical and electronic equipment who sell their products in the EU to operate a recycling program. Waste electrical and electronic equipment (i.e. equipment that has reached the end of its useful life) contains a lot of valuable materials. Manufacturers are required to set up a system in Europe to accept waste electrical and electronic equipment from any source and arrange for the appropriate disposal or recycling of that product.

Recycling electronic and electrical equipment

Environmental pollution

We must all take responsibility for the environment through conscientious use, recycling of equipment and minimising the use of electricity and consumables such as paper and toner.

Fact: Global data centres used roughly 416 terawatts (4.16×10^{14} watts) of electricity in 2017, almost 40% more than the entire UK. This consumption is set to double every four years.

Exercises

1. "All organisations and individuals have a moral obligation to take action to preserve the planet for future generations."

   (a) Explain **one** reason why you agree or disagree with this statement. [2]

   (b) Explain **two** ways in which technology is harmful to the environment. [4]

   (c) Describe **two** steps that an organisation can take to minimise environmental damage caused by the use of technology. [4]

2. "Lack of connectivity is a major cause of digital exclusion."

   Describe **two** other factors that contribute to unequal access to IT for people in the UK. [4]

3. A MOOC (Massive Open Online Course) is an online course aimed at unlimited participation and open access via the web. There are thousands of MOOCs available on the Internet.

   (a) Describe **two** potential benefits of these courses for teenagers and adults wishing to learn about aspects of technology. [4]

   (b) Describe **two** reasons why students in developing countries may not be able to take advantage of these courses. [4]

Chapter 32
Current legislation

Objectives

- Describe the role of current legislation (and subsequent additions and amendments) in protecting users and their data from attack or misuse

Current legislation

Crime is a feature of every society. As technology develops, new crimes emerge; the first computer virus was released in 1986. Until a few years ago, viruses and other malware were used to conduct isolated acts of vandalism or anti-social behaviour and were confined to infecting a few hard disks or programs.

Today, cybercrime is a major concern, with the criminal underworld realising the huge opportunities for making money both from their own malware and from writing malware for sale to others.

> **Q1** What has been one of the key factors over the past 30 years leading to the rise, extent and seriousness of computer crime?

In response to any type of crime, society attempts to find ways to prevent the crime and to punish the perpetrators. This means, first of all, creating legislation to make specific activities illegal.

Computer Misuse Act 1990

The first piece of UK legislation designed to specifically address computer misuse was the Computer Misuse Act 1990. This Act was a response to growing concern that existing legislation was inadequate for dealing with hackers.

This law makes the following activities illegal:

- Unauthorised access to computer material (penalty: up to two years in prison and a fine)
- Unauthorised access with intent to commit further offences (penalty: up to 5 years in prison and a fine)
- Unauthorised modification of computer material (penalty: up to 10 years in prison and a fine)

Under this law, it is an offence to access someone else's computer or data without their permission.

> **Q2** List some specific activities which are illegal under this law.

Spam is something that almost everyone with an email account has to deal with regularly. While spam is a nuisance, wasting bandwidth and delivering unwanted content, it is not in itself illegal. However, it is often used to deliver malware, and is the most common method used in phishing attacks to direct victims to fake web sites from which confidential data is then extracted.

Police and Justice Act 2006

Legislation sometimes cannot keep up with new offences made possible by technological advancement. In November 2004, a teenager was accused of bringing down a server by sending millions of emails. However, as he had not technically made unauthorised changes to a computer, he had not breached the Computer Misuse Act and he was found not guilty of any offence. (This ruling was overturned in 2006.)

The **Police and Justice Act 2006** was largely concerned with policing reform but included amendments to the **Computer Misuse Act**.

- The maximum prison sentence under Section 1 of the original Act ("unauthorised access") was increased from six months to two years.

- Section 3 of the Act ("unauthorised modification of computer material") was amended to read "unauthorised acts with intent to impair or with recklessness as to impairing, operation of computer, etc." and carries a maximum sentence of ten years.

- A further section, "making, supplying or obtaining articles for use in computer misuse offences" was added, carrying a maximum sentence of two years.

Computer misuse may result in a prison sentence

What particular type of serious malware attack was made illegal, with a maximum sentence of 10 years, by Section 3 of this Act?

Protecting users and their data

Legislation is important in defining what constitutes criminal behaviour and ensuring that those who are caught committing cybercrimes are appropriately punished. This is one area in which joint policing operations across national borders, and international legislation across the globe, is needed to combat cybercrime, which knows no borders.

Educating individuals and organisations so that they understand the risks and have the knowledge and tools to minimise their exposure to cybercrime is essential. Many individuals are technically inexperienced and have a very limited awareness of the potential dangers of online shopping, Internet banking and social networking. Imaginative and varied ways of raising awareness of cybercrime are needed to reduce the probability of becoming a victim.

Copyright, Designs and Patents Act 1988

This Act is not specific to computer material. It gives the creators of literary, dramatic, musical and artistic works the right to control the ways in which their material may be used.

Literary, dramatic, musical or artistic works and films are covered for 70 years after the creator's death. Sound recordings and broadcasts are covered for 50 years after the last remaining creator dies.

Copyright (Computer Programs) Regulations 1992

The 1988 Copyright Act also applies to software. The 1992 regulations harmonised the law across the EU and included matters for which the Act made no specific provision or makes a different provision.

When you buy software, it is illegal to:

- make a copy and sell it or give it to a friend
- use software on a network unless the licence allows it

It is, however, legal to make back-up copies of programs when using them lawfully.

All kinds of technological works that are used with computers, tablets, smartphones, or video game systems are covered by Copyright law. Apps, computer programs, databases, spreadsheets, screen displays, and virtual reality environments are all covered. The law also applies to works that are used or distributed on the Internet such as websites, blogs, and other online content.

Fair dealing

The copyright laws of almost all countries allow exceptions for certain permitted uses of copyrighted works such as news reporting or educational uses. Legitimate uses include:

- private study and research
- making a backup copy of software or data for personal use

Fair dealing includes using copyright material in private study and research

Health and Safety (Display Screen Equipment) Regulations 1992

The main provisions are:

- Employers must carry out a risk assessment of workstations used by employees to reduce any identified risks.

- Employers must ensure that employees take regular and adequate breaks from looking at their screens.

- Employers must ensure that employees are aware of their entitlement to yearly eye tests, with the cost of the eye test met by the employer in full.

- Employers must provide their computer users with adequate health and safety training for any workstation they work at.

Assessment of workstations

A risk assessment for screen use could include:

- ensuring that lighting in the room does not cause glare or reflections in the screen caused by light from a window behind the screen

- checking that screens do not flicker, and text is of an appropriate size

- ensuring that screens are kept clean and dust-free

Regular reviews should be carried out when staff or equipment changes are made, to prevent potential RSI and other health problems arising.

Correct sitting posture at workstation

Data Protection Act 2018

The new Data Protection Act came into force in May 2018, replacing the previous Act of 1998. It is aligned with the **General Data Protection Regulation** (**GDPR**), agreed upon by the European Parliament and Council in April 2016 and introduced in May 2018 across the European Union.

All organisations holding or processing personal information must make sure that it is:

- used fairly, lawfully and transparently

- used for specified, explicit purposes

- used in a way that is adequate, relevant and limited to only what is necessary

- accurate and, where necessary, kept up to date

- kept for no longer than is necessary

- handled in a way that ensures appropriate security, including protection against unlawful or unauthorised processing, access, loss, destruction or damage

The individual's rights

Under the Data Protection Act 2018, you have the right to find out what information the Government and other organisations store about you. This includes the right to:

- be informed about how your data is being used
- access personal data
- have incorrect data updated
- have data erased
- stop or restrict the processing of your data
- data portability (allowing you to get and reuse your data for different services)
- object to how your data is processed in certain circumstances

Consumer Rights Act 2015

Under this Act all products, whether digital or physical, must meet the following standards:

- satisfactory quality – not faulty or damaged (taking into account, for example, that bargain basement products won't be held to as high standards as luxury goods)
- fit for purpose – for the purpose they are supplied for, or any purpose you made known to the retailer when you bought them
- as described – matching any description given to you or samples shown to you at time of purchase

Exercises

1. (a) Jason is a student at Hillcrest College. He is submitting a piece of written work which will be sent to the Exam Board as part of the requirements of his course. He has copied (plagiarised) someone else's work from an essay posted on the Web.

    Explain **one** method by which an examiner may use technology to detect plagiarism. [2]

   (b) Mina is a research student at University who is submitting a paper to a scientific journal.

    Describe **two** reasons why the Copyright, Designs and Patents Act (1988) may be relevant to her submission. [4]

2. A bank offers advice to customers about how to stay safe online. Describe information or advice they might include under the headings:

   (a) Suspicious messages [4]

   (b) Protecting your devices [4]

3. Tony is the manager of a small business with several employees using desktop computers.

    Describe **four** measures that Tony should take to ensure that he meets the requirements of the Health and Safety (Display Screen Equipment) Regulations 1992. [8]

Chapter 33
Moral and ethical factors in the use of IT systems

Objectives

- Consider some of the moral and ethical issues arising from the use of information technology
- Describe the purpose and role of codes of practice produced by professional bodies for the use of IT systems
- Describe the impact of codes of practice on individuals and organisations

Ethics vs Morals – what's the difference?

Ethics and morals are both concerned with what is the 'right' behaviour in different circumstances.

- Ethics are defined by rules decided by an external source, for example an Acceptable Use Policy or a Code of Conduct applicable to different professions or organisations.
- Morals refer to an individual's own principles.

Ethics	Morals
Rules of conduct recognised within a particular group, culture or profession	Personal compass of right and wrong conduct
Ethics are proscribed by a social system or the rules of a profession	Morals are individual
We follow ethical guidelines because society says it is the right thing to do	Our morals tell us whether something is right or wrong, regardless of rules
A person can follow ethical principles but have no morals at all	A moral person usually also follows an applicable code of ethics
Ethics are governed by professional and legal guidelines in a particular time, place or context	Morality is universal

Organisations commonly monitor employees' activities at work.

(a) Do they have a moral obligation to notify employees of the extent of this monitoring?

(b) If the organisation notifies employees that they should have no expectation of privacy when using the email system, is it an ethical violation when employees later find out that a manager was actually reading their e-mails?

The use of algorithms

Almost without our realising it, our world has become dominated by algorithms. From digital cameras which automatically focus on a smiling face, to the complex algorithms used in driverless cars, many of the decisions we used to have to make ourselves are now made for us by algorithms.

Profiling and classification algorithms determine how individuals and groups are managed. Artificial Intelligence has greatly increased the ability of organisations to exploit people. Users may be given recommendations on how to exercise, what to buy and who to buy from.

Tech firms can extract meaning from the data unwittingly handed over when using a search engine or a social media site. Retailers can now track customers via their smartphones and record which stores they visit. They can also gather data on what catches a customer's eye as they move around the store and which displays they walk straight past.

Detailed knowledge and analysis of consumer behaviour gathered in this way can lead to consumers paying more for particular items. Is this practice ethical?

Your smartphone can track your movements around a store

Case study: Should Google accept Viagogo advertisements?

Google has been urged to stop accepting money from Viagogo to place the ticket website at the top of its search rankings, in an open letter signed by the Football Association, several MPs and the trade body UK Music.

The letter, sent to senior Google executives says that Viagogo's prominence in search rankings is leading to consumers buying sports, music and theatre tickets that may be invalid.

The letter also expressed concern that fans are being directed to the site, where tickets are sold at vast markups, even when face-value tickets are still on sale elsewhere.

The UK website of Viagogo, which has faced a barrage of criticism for controversial business practices, derives 75% of its website traffic from search engine referrals.

Labour MP Sharon Hodgson, one of the letter's signatories, said: "*I have heard too many times from distressed customers of Viagogo that they were led to the website because it was at the top of their Google search. It is totally wrong that a trusted website like Google would direct consumers to such an untrustworthy website.*

"*Google needs to take action in order to protect consumers, and I look forward to working with them on this in the very near future.*"

Discuss the ethics of both Google and Viagogo highlighted by this case study.

Codes of practice

A code of practice is a set of written guidelines issued by a professional body, setting out how people working in a particular profession should behave.

The British Computer Society (BCS) issues a Code of Conduct for its members. It applies to all members working in IT, whether as academics, employees, contractors or independent consultants.

The BCS Code of Conduct

This lists guidelines for people working in IT:

1. Maintain your technical competence
2. Adhere to regulations
3. Act professionally as a specialist
4. Use appropriate methods and tools
5. Manage your workload efficiently
6. Participate maturely
7. Respect the interests of your customers
8. Promote good practices within the organisation
9. Represent the profession to the public

A Code of Good Practice encourages cooperation among employees

Impact on individuals

A code of practice is a guide and reference for employees.

- It encourages cooperation between employees, and good customer relations.
- It motivates employees who know they are working for a good company that cares about its employees.
- Employees can legitimately ask for permission to attend courses to 'maintain technical competence'.

Impact on organisations

A code of practice is important for an organisation for several reasons, including the following:

- Compliance: Legislation requires individuals on company boards to implement codes of practice or explain why they have not.

- Marketing: A code serves as a public statement of what the company stands for and its commitment to high standards and the right conduct.

- Ethics: A code encourages discussions of ethics and compliance, empowering employees to handle ethical dilemmas they encounter in everyday work.

- Employee reviews: It can serve as a reference document in regular reviews of employee performance.

Exercises

1. ITQ is a company which sells information based on an analysis of publicly available data on a social media site intended for people to connect for professional reasons. The profile data is collected by bots, which gather information from the site according to parameters provided. The information is gathered whenever new information is posted, and this information is organised and interpreted by ITQ's software.

   The software can:

   - analyse employee skills
   - identify employees at risk of being recruited away

   (a) Describe **two** reasons why an employer might pay ITQ for this type of data. [4]

   (b) Describe **two** reasons why employees might be concerned about this data being collected and distributed without their permission or knowledge. [4]

   (c) A social media site went to court to try to stop ITQ from using user data in this way, but the judge ruled it was not illegal.

   Explain why some people may nevertheless regard the activities of ITQ as unethical. [4]

2. AC Software is a company producing accounting software used by thousands of small companies. The company follows a code of conduct produced by the British Computer Society for the use of IT systems.

   (a) Describe the **purpose** of the code of conduct in an organisation. [4]

   (b) Describe **three impacts** of the code of conduct on the employees of AC Software. [6]

Chapter 34
Equality and accessibility

Objectives

- Describe guidelines and current legislation designed to ensure the accessibility of IT systems

What is accessibility?

In this context it refers to the accessibility of a computer system by all people, regardless of disability, type or severity of impairment. Making an IT system accessible may involve providing specialised hardware, software, or a combination of both, designed to enable use by a person with a disability or impairment.

A wide range of accessibility devices is available, some of which are described in Section A.

Creating IT systems that meet users' needs will result in:

- increased job satisfaction
- improved morale
- increased productivity

for everyone, including people with disabilities.

An organisation can build a reputation for being accessible to everyone, including people with special needs.

Barriers to effective use

Computer users may be affected by any of a range of disabilities including:

- complete or partial blindness
- colour blindness
- hearing-related disabilities
- motor or dexterity impairment such as paralysis, cerebral palsy, or repetitive strain injury (RSI)
- cognitive impairments such as head injury, autism, or learning disabilities such as dyslexia or ADHD

A blind or partially-sighted person can listen to an audio book using an audio book player

Different settings available in an operating system

Operating systems such as Windows have built-in accessibility options which can be turned on. Some of these are specifically designed to make it possible or easier for someone with a particular disability to use a computer effectively.

Typing "Ease of access" in the Search bar will display the available options.

Accessibility options in Windows 10 operating system

Equality Act 2010

The **Equality Act 2010** legally protects people from discrimination in the workplace and in wider society. It replaced previous anti-discrimination laws with a single Act, incorporating and replacing the **Disability Discrimination Acts 1995** and **2005** which have now been repealed. Under the new Act, as under the previous one, organisations are obliged to make necessary adjustments for disabled employees and job applicants. This includes provision of specialised hardware and software if required.

The Act also placed further obligations on website owners and hosts to ensure sites are accessible. This might include:

- making the site accessible without using a mouse
- adding alternative text to images
- using a consistent layout and structure
- avoiding poor contrast
- breaking up text into meaningful sections
- providing an accessibility page
- performing an accessibility check using free online software

Open Accessibility Framework (OAF)

The framework is designed to help website and application developers create accessible websites and applications.

The six steps to the framework are:

Step 1: Defining what 'accessible' means: Navigation schemes, good colour contrast, large print

Step 2: Having accessible stock interface elements ready to go: Desktop menus, windows, sliders etc

Step 3: Develop authoring tools: Manuals and tutorials, palette of sample elements

Step 4: Platform support: User selectable themes

Step 5: The App itself: Make accessible applications

Step 6: Assistive technology: Provide screen readers, keyboard alternatives, etc.

Web Content Accessibility Guidelines (WCAG 2.1)

Guidelines are given on how to make content more accessible to people with disabilities including:

- blindness and low vision: text alternatives can be given for non-text content such as images or graphs. All the text can then be spoken.

- deafness and hearing loss: text transcriptions may be provided for videos and audio-only content. On some websites, sign language interpretation may be provided.

- limited movement: for example, all functionality is made operable through a keyboard interface for users who cannot easily control a mouse.

- speech disabilities: speech input is not required, or an alternative input method is provided.

Descriptive text can be spoken

 Describe one way a spreadsheet can be made accessible to a partially-sighted person.

World Wide Web Consortium

Known as W3C, this organisation was established in 1994 by the creator of the Web, Sir Tim Berners-Lee. Its stated mission is "to lead the World Wide Web to its full potential by developing protocols and guidelines that ensure the long-term growth of the Web".

Sir Tim Berners-Lee, founder of the World Wide Web, Orlando Florida January 2018

British Standards Institute

The British Standards Institute (BSI) is a service organisation that produces standards across a wide variety of industry sectors. It publishes Codes of Practice for Web accessibility, similar to those shown on page 181 for WCAG 2.1.

Exercises

1. (a) Describe what is meant by **accessibility** in the context of information technology.   [2]

    (b) Ray is colour blind.

    Describe **one** way that a website designer can ensure that no text is unreadable by him.   [2]

    (c) Rihanna is blind.

    Describe **two** specialised hardware devices that Rihanna may need in order to use IT effectively.   [4]

2. (a) Describe the purpose of the Open Accessibility Framework (OAF).   [2]

    (b) Describe **two** steps in the framework designed to help achieve its purpose.   [4]

Index

CPSIA information can be obtained
at www.ICGtesting.com
Printed in the USA
BVHW021323160922
647217BV00012B/264